Ch

DAT

CONTEMPORARY
ISSUES
COMPANION

Child Abuse

Other Books of Related Interest:

Opposing Viewpoints Series

Adoption

America's Youth

The Catholic Church

Child Abuse

Education

The Family

Juvenile Crime

Teenage Pregnancy

Welfare

Current Controversies Series

Drug Abuse

Family Violence

Issues in Adoption

Teen Pregnancy and Parenting

Violence Against Women

Youth Violence

At Issue Series

Child Labor and Sweatshops

Child Sexual Abuse

Child Sexual Abuse in the Catholic Church

Do Children Have Rights?

Violent Children

CONTEMPORARY
ISSUES
COMPANION

Child Abuse

Jean Leverich, Book Editor

GREENHAVEN PRESS

An imprint of Thomson Gale, a part of The Thomson Corporation

THOMSON
GALE

Detroit • New York • San Francisco • San Diego • New Haven, Conn.
Waterville, Maine • London • Munich

Bonnie Szumski, *Publisher*
Helen Cothran, *Managing Editor*
David M. Haugen, *Series Editor*

© 2006 Thomson Gale, a part of The Thomson Corporation.

Thomson and Star Logo are trademarks and Gale and Greenhaven Press are registered trade-marks used herein under license.

For more information, contact:
Greenhaven Press
27500 Drake Rd.
Farmington Hills, MI 48331-3535
Or you can visit our Internet site at http://www.gale.com

LIBRARY OF CONGRESS CATALOGING-IN-PUBLICATION DATA

Child Abuse / Jean Leverich, book editor
    p. cm. -- (Contemporary issues companion)
    Includes bibliographical references and index.
0-7377-3247-4 (lib. bdg. : alk. paper) 0-7377-3248-2 (pbk. : alk. paper)
  1. Child abuse--United States. 2. Abused children--United States--Interviews.
3. Child abuse--United States--Prevention. I. Leverich, Jean Marie. II. Series.
  HV6626.52.C54 2006
  362.760973--dc22

                                                         2005056278

Printed in the United States of America
10 9 8 7 6 5 4 3 2 1

Contents

Foreword

In the news, on the streets, and in neighborhoods, individuals are confronted with a variety of social problems. Such problems may affect people directly: A young woman may struggle with depression, suspect a friend of having bulimia, or watch a loved one battle cancer. And even the issues that do not directly affect her private life—such as religious cults, domestic violence, or legalized gambling—still impact the larger society in which she lives. Discovering and analyzing the complexities of issues that encompass communal and societal realms as well as the world of personal experience is a valuable educational goal in the modern world.

Effectively addressing social problems requires familiarity with a constantly changing stream of data. Becoming well informed about today's controversies is an intricate process that often involves reading myriad primary and secondary sources, analyzing political debates, weighing various experts' opinions—even listening to firsthand accounts of those directly affected by the issue. For students and general observers, this can be a daunting task because of the sheer volume of information available in books, periodicals, on the evening news, and on the Internet. Researching the consequences of legalized gambling, for example, might entail sifting through congressional testimony on gambling's societal effects, examining private studies on Indian gaming, perusing numerous Web sites devoted to Internet betting, and reading essays written by lottery winners as well as interviews with recovering compulsive gamblers. Obtaining valuable information can be time-consuming—since it often requires researchers to pore over numerous documents and commentaries before discovering a source relevant to their particular investigation.

Greenhaven's Contemporary Issues Companion series seeks to assist this process of research by providing readers with useful and pertinent information about today's complex issues. Each volume in this anthology series focuses on a topic of current interest, presenting informative and thought-provoking selections written from a wide variety of viewpoints. The readings selected by the editors include such diverse sources as personal accounts and case studies, pertinent factual and statistical articles, and relevant commentaries and overviews. This diversity of sources and views, found in every Contemporary Issues Companion, offers readers a broad perspective in one convenient volume.

In addition, each title in the Contemporary Issues Companion series is designed especially for young adults. The selections included in every volume are chosen for their accessibility and are expertly edited in consideration of both the reading and comprehension levels of the audience. The structure of the anthologies also enhances accessibility. An introductory essay places each issue in context and provides helpful facts such as historical background or current statistics and legislation that pertain to the topic. The chapters that follow organize the material and focus on specific aspects of the book's topic. Every essay is introduced by a brief summary of its main points and biographical information about the author. These summaries aid in comprehension and can also serve to direct readers to material of immediate interest and need. Finally, a comprehensive index allows readers to efficiently scan and locate content.

The Contemporary Issues Companion series is an ideal launching point for research on a particular topic. Each anthology in the series is composed of readings taken from an extensive gamut of resources, including periodicals, newspapers, books, government documents, the publications of private and public organizations, and Internet Web sites. In these volumes, readers will find factual support suitable for use in reports, debates, speeches, and research papers. The anthologies also facilitate further research, featuring a book and periodical bibliography and a list of organizations to contact for additional information.

A perfect resource for both students and the general reader, Greenhaven's Contemporary Issues Companion series is sure to be a valued source of current, readable information on social problems that interest young adults. It is the editors' hope that readers will find the Contemporary Issues Companion series useful as a starting point to formulate their own opinions about and answers to the complex issues of the present day.

Introduction

On January 4, 2003, seven-year-old Raheem Williams and his four-year-old brother, Tyrone, were found locked in a Newark, New Jersey, basement. The brothers were hiding under a bed, severely dehydrated and malnourished, lying in their own waste, their hair covered with lice. After Raheem told police on the scene that his twin brother was missing, officers searched the house and found the emaciated body of Faheem Williams in a sealed, plastic container hidden deep within a closet. Faheem had died of starvation and blunt trauma to his stomach. The surviving brothers were hospitalized. The boys had been abandoned by their mother, Melinda Williams, who had left the unwanted children in the care of a series of relatives. The children had never attended school and had no medical or dental records. A relative reported that Melinda had told her, long after Faheem died, that she had "never liked" Faheem and preferred Raheem. Another relative told reporters that although the children were often hungry, she did not believe that Melinda beat them.

"The family was known to the department for ten years. There were indications that this was a family in trouble and the children were at risk," Gwendolyn Harris, commissioner of the New Jersey Department of Human Services, told the Newark, New Jersey, *Star-Ledger*. "Clearly, something in the system failed." Before Faheem's death, the family had come to the attention of the New Jersey Division of Youth and Family Services (DYFS) at least eleven times, but the children were never removed from their mother's home. At the time, the average caseload for caseworkers at New Jersey's DYFS was thirty-five, well above the twenty-five cases recommended by national advocates. In February 2002 DYFS closed the Williams case despite open allegations of abuse and neglect, because the worker could not find the family. The next time the family was heard from, seven-year-old Faheem was dead.

The tragic case of the Williams children made national news—and brought public scrutiny upon New Jersey's antiquated, underfunded, and overwhelmed child welfare agency. However, child neglect—unless it is fatal or near fatal—does not capture the public's attention in the way that child sexual abuse or child abduction do. Deborah Daro, an expert on child abuse prevention at the University of Chicago, calls child neglect "the most forgotten" form of child abuse. "The neglect of neglect" is a phrase coined by social workers Isabel Wolock and Bernard Horowitz to describe the disinterest exhibited by academics, child abuse prevention workers, and the general public in the topic when compared to other forms of child abuse.

Child neglect generally refers to a failure to meet a child's basic needs. There are three basic categories of neglect— physical, educational or developmental, and emotional. Within those main categories, at least eleven types of child neglect have been consistently described: health care or medical neglect, personal hygiene neglect, nutritional neglect, neglect of household safety, neglect of household sanitation, inadequate shelter, abandonment, supervisory neglect, educational neglect, emotional neglect, and fostering delinquency. The Williams boys were victims of multiple forms of extreme neglect: nutritional neglect to the point of starvation; abandonment by their mother and then by a series of relatives in whose care they were placed; supervisory neglect, as they were left on their own in the basement for days on end; emotional neglect, expressed in one instance, by Melinda Williams's claim that she did not like Faheem; and the medical and educational neglect reflected in the children's lack of medical, dental, and school records.

Despite the lack of interest among academics, clinicians, and the general public, neglect is by far the most common form of child abuse reported. According to statistics gathered by the Department of Health and Human Services (DHHS), in 2003, of the 906,000 children determined to be victims of child abuse, more than 60 percent suffered from neglect, while 20 percent were victims of physical abuse, and not quite 10 percent were sexually abused (the remaining percent were emotionally abused, medically neglected, and "other"). During 2003 an estimated 1,500 children died from abuse or neglect—a rate of 2 deaths per 100,000 children. The DHHS reports that more than one-third (35.6 percent) of those deaths were from child neglect alone.

If child neglect is more common than physical and sexual abuse, why then is it the least often discussed? Howard Dubowitz, professor of pediatrics and director of the Center for Child Protection at the University of Maryland Medical Center, suggests six reasons for inattention to child neglect. First, Dubowitz contends, many people believe that neglect often does not result in serious consequences; second, many people feel it is inappropriate to judge neglectful parents when poverty is a contributing issue; third, child neglect, like poverty and racism, seems an insurmountable problem; fourth, many people believe that other forms of maltreatment, such as sexual and physical abuse, are more damaging and therefore more compelling; fifth, the definition of neglect is ambiguous and it is therefore difficult to say precisely when a behavior constitutes neglect; and sixth, thinking about child neglect provokes negative feelings that people would rather avoid.

Although child neglect does have serious consequences, the effects of child neglect are usually incremental, and therefore it is more difficult to observe child neglect unless a case worker or educator has multiple encounters with a child and his or her family. A 1994 study by social workers Brian Minty and Graham Pattinson suggests that heavy caseloads lead child protective service workers to neglect cases of neglect. That is, with limited staff and resources, it is difficult for workers to systematically collect evidence over a period of time in order to establish that a child is neglected. Studies have also found that child protective service workers will sometimes minimize the seriousness of neglect by labeling it "normal" for a particular ethnic group or by assuming an "optimistic" viewpoint in which they assume that the parents' love will mitigate the consequences of the neglect.

The belief that it is inappropriate to judge poor families who neglect their children and that neglect, like poverty, is an insurmountable problem, is a large barrier to confronting the problem of child neglect, both on individual and policy levels. According to 2003 statistics from DHHS, the strongest predictor for neglect is socioeconomic status. The neglect of child neglect is thus inexorably tied to the larger neglect of the poor in the United States. Like neglect, poverty in America is largely invisible, especially in terms of media coverage. Psychologist Michael J. Bader notes that "The children imperiled by neglect, indifference and poverty don't appear on milk cartons, they aren't plastered on the front pages of our newspapers, or appear as the lead story on CNN."

African American and Hispanic children are overrepresented in the DHHS statistics on neglect because minority children are significantly poorer than Caucasian children in the United States. As social workers Margaret G. Smith and Rowena Fong write in *The Children of Neglect: When No One Cares*, poor children are much more likely to live in substandard housing, live in violent neighborhoods, receive substandard education, have limited or no access to health care, or be hungry than the children of the comfortable. The parents of poor children are more likely to be less educated, to be unemployed or underemployed, to be less healthy themselves, to have higher levels of stress, and to have less access to reliable transportation or child care than the parents of wealthy or middle-class children.

The enormity of the problem of neglect and poverty is further compounded by lack of consensus over what forms of parenting are dangerous or unacceptable, as well as uncertainty about whether to define maltreatment based on adult characteristics, adult behavior, child behavior, the child's environment, or some combination of these. Although the story of the Williams children is a horrifying and extreme example of neglect, experts and the public generally acknowledge that all parents are occasionally neglectful of their children's physical and emotional needs. If a child were to occasionally miss a meal or skip a bath, for example, few people would accuse a parent of neglect; however, as Ola Barnett, professor of psychology at Pepperdine University, suggests, a child who misses many meals and seldom bathes is neglected. According to Barnett, a continuum exists between ideal child care and child neglect. Additionally, because neglect is about omission—about things not done, it is more difficult to describe and detect than physical or sexual abuse. Therefore, neglect can seem less obviously "deviant" than physically or sexually hurting a child. Barnett contends that it is this lack of apparent deviance along a continuum of behavior that makes society uncomfortable with child neglect. Because it is sometimes difficult to determine at what point less-than-adequate parenting or a parental mistake becomes neglect requiring intervention, people are hesitant to act.

Because socioeconomic status is the largest predictor of abuse, several researchers and practitioners hold that neglect will not be adequately addressed until the government implements policy and public health strategies that prioritize children's well-being, address the causes of poverty, and consider child neglect a major threat to public health. In addition to providing for children's safety and teaching parenting skills to neglectful families, they contend, the social context that leads to neglect must be changed. The best way to prevent neglect is to ensure adequate child care, income, health care, housing, safe neighborhoods, employment programs, and other resources to support families under stress.

The controversy surrounding child neglect and how best to support at-risk children and their families is one of the issues examined in *Child Abuse: Contemporary Issues Companion*. In the chapters that follow, discussions focus on the history and causes of child abuse, the prevention of child victimization, and the personal narratives of survivors of child abuse. These essays provide a comprehensive overview of one of the most disturbing issues facing American society today.

CHAPTER 1

The Scope of Child Abuse in America

The Definition of Child Abuse

Jill Goldman and Marsha K. Salus

In the following selection, authors Jill Goldman and Marsha K. Salus define the four main forms of child abuse, which they label physical abuse, sexual abuse, neglect, and psychological or emotional abuse. Although the federal government provides minimum standards for defining child abuse, through the Child Abuse Prevention and Treatment Act (CAPTA), the authors note that each state is responsible for providing its own definitions of child maltreatment within civil and criminal contexts. The federal and state definitions of child abuse guide Child Protective Services (CPS) workers when they investigate allegations of abuse.

Jill Goldman has served as manager of product development and program services for the National Clearinghouse on Child Abuse and Neglect Information, and has written extensively on child maltreatment and other issues concerning children, youth, and families. Marsha K. Salus has worked in the child welfare field for thirty years. She has consulted with several states to establish uniform standards of practice for child welfare workers.

To prevent and respond to child abuse and neglect effectively, there needs to be a common understanding of the definitions of those actions and omissions that constitute child maltreatment. Unfortunately, there is no single, universally applied definition of child abuse and neglect. Over the past several decades, different stakeholders—including State and Federal legislative bodies, agency officials, and researchers—have developed definitions of maltreatment for different purposes. Definitions vary across these groups and within them. For example, legal definitions describing the different forms of child maltreatment for reporting and criminal prosecution purposes are found mainly in State statutes, and defi-

Jill Goldman and Marsha K. Salus, *A Coordinated Response to Child Abuse and Neglect: The Foundation for Practice*. Washington, DC: U.S. Department of Health and Human Services, 2003.

nitions vary from State to State. Similarly, agency guidelines for accepting reports, conducting investigations, and providing interventions vary from State to State and sometimes from county to county. In addition, researchers use varying methods to measure and define abuse and neglect, making it difficult to compare findings across studies. Despite the differences, there are commonalities across definitions. . . .

Federal Definitions of Child Abuse

The Child Abuse Prevention and Treatment Act (CAPTA) provides minimum standards for defining physical child abuse, child neglect, and sexual abuse that States must incorporate in their statutory definitions to receive Federal funds. Under CAPTA, child abuse and neglect means:

- Any recent act or failure to act on the part of a parent or caretaker that results in death, serious physical or emotional harm, sexual abuse, or exploitation;

- An act or failure to act that presents an imminent risk of serious harm.

The definition of child abuse and neglect refers specifically to parents and other caregivers. A "child" under this definition generally means a person who is under the age of 18 or who is not an emancipated minor. In cases of child sexual abuse, a "child" is one who has not attained the age of 18 or the age specified by the child protection law of the State in which the child resides, whichever is younger. . . .

State Definitions of Child Abuse

While the Federal legislation sets minimum definitional standards, each State is responsible for providing its own definition of maltreatment within civil and criminal contexts. The problem of child maltreatment is generally subject to State laws (both statutes and case law) and administrative regulations. Definitions of child abuse and neglect are located primarily in three places within each State's statutory code:

- *Mandatory child maltreatment reporting statutes (civil laws)* provide definitions of child maltreatment to guide those individuals mandated to identify and report suspected child abuse. These reports activate the child protection process. . . .

- *Criminal statutes* define those forms of child maltreatment that are criminally punishable. In most jurisdictions, child maltreatment is criminally punishable when one or more of the following statutory crimes have been committed: homicide, murder, manslaughter, false imprisonment, assault, battery, criminal neglect and abandonment, emotional and physical abuse, child pornography, child prostitution, computer crimes, rape, deviant sexual assault, indecent exposure, child endangerment, and reckless endangerment.

- *Juvenile court jurisdiction statutes* provide definitions of the circumstances necessary for the court to have jurisdiction over a child alleged to have been abused or neglected. When the child's safety cannot be ensured in the home, these statutes allow the court to take custody of a child and to order specific treatment services for the parents and child. Together, these legal definitions of child abuse and neglect determine the minimum standards of care and protection for children and serve as important guidelines for professionals regarding those acts and omissions that constitute child maltreatment.

Child protective services (CPS) workers use statutory definitions of child maltreatment to determine whether maltreatment has occurred and when intervention into family life is necessary. For particular localities within a State, local CPS policies and procedures, based on statutes and regulations, further define different types of maltreatment and the conditions under which intervention and services are warranted.

Types of Child Abuse

There are four commonly recognized forms of child abuse or maltreatment:

- Physical
- Sexual
- Neglect
- Psychological

There is great variation from State to State regarding the details and specificity of child abuse definitions, but it is still possible to identify commonalities among each different type of child maltreatment. These commonalities, in part, reflect societal views of parental actions that are seen as improper or unacceptable because they place children at a risk of physical and emotional harm.

Physical Abuse

Generally, physical abuse is characterized by physical injury, such as bruises and fractures that result from:

- Punching
- Beating
- Kicking
- Biting
- Shaking
- Throwing
- Stabbing
- Choking
- Hitting with a hand, stick, strap, or other object
- Burning

Although an injury resulting from physical abuse is not accidental, the parent or caregiver may not have intended to hurt the child. The injury may have resulted from severe discipline, including injurious spanking, or physical punishment that is inappropriate to the child's age or condition. The injury may be the result of a single episode or of repeated episodes and can range in severity from minor marks and bruising to death.

Some cultural practices are generally not defined as physical abuse, but may result in physically hurting children. For example:

- "Coining" or *cao gio*—a practice to treat illness by rubbing the body forcefully with a coin or other hard object.

- *Moxabustion*—an Asian folkloric remedy that burns the skin.

As Howard Dubowitz, a leading researcher in the field, explains [in *Handbook for Child Protection Practice* (2000)]: "While cultural practices are generally respected, if the injury or harm is significant, professionals typically work with parents to discourage harmful behavior and suggest preferable alternatives."

Sexual Abuse

Child sexual abuse generally refers to sexual acts, sexually motivated behaviors involving children, or sexual exploitation of children. Child sexual abuse includes a wide range of behaviors, such as:

- Oral, anal, or genital penile penetration;

- Anal or genital digital or other penetration;

- Genital contact with no intrusion;

- Fondling of a child's breasts or buttocks;

- Indecent exposure;

- Inadequate or inappropriate supervision of a child's voluntary sexual activities;

- Use of a child in prostitution, pornography, Internet crimes, or other sexually exploitative activities.

Sexual abuse includes both touching offenses (fondling or sexual intercourse) and nontouching offenses (exposing a child to pornographic materials) and can involve varying degrees of violence and emotional trauma. The most commonly reported cases involve incest—sexual abuse occurring among family members, including those in biological families, adoptive families, and step-families. Incest most often occurs within a father-daughter relationship; however, mother-son, father-son, and sibling-sibling incest also occurs. Sexual abuse is also sometimes committed by other relatives or caretakers, such as aunts, uncles, grandparents, cousins, or the boyfriend or girlfriend of a parent.

Child Neglect

Child neglect, the most common form of child maltreatment, is generally characterized by omissions in care resulting in significant harm or risk of significant harm. Neglect is frequently defined in terms of a failure to provide for the child's basic needs—deprivation of adequate food, clothing, shelter, supervision, or medical care. Neglect laws often exclude circumstances in which a child's needs are not met because of poverty or an inability to provide. In addition, many States establish religious exemptions for parents who choose not to seek medical care for their children due to religious beliefs that may prohibit medical intervention.

The Department of Health and Human Services' *Third National Incidence Study of Child Abuse and Neglect* (NIS-3) [(1996)] is the single most comprehensive source of information about the current incidence of child maltreatment in the United States. NIS-3 worked with researchers and practitioners to define physical, educational, and emotional neglect in a succinct and clear manner, as described below.

Kinds of Child Neglect

Physical Neglect

- *Refusal of health care*—the failure to provide or allow needed care in accordance with recommendations of a competent health care professional for a physical injury, illness, medical condition, or impairment.

- *Delay in health care*—the failure to seek timely and appropriate medical care for a serious health problem that any reasonable layman would have recognized as needing professional medical attention.

- *Abandonment*—the desertion of a child without arranging for reasonable care and supervision.

- *Expulsion*—other blatant refusals of custody, such as permanent or indefinite expulsion of a child from the home without adequate arrangement for care by others or refusal to accept custody of a returned runaway.

- *Inadequate supervision*—leaving a child unsupervised or inadequately supervised for extended periods of time or allowing the child to remain away from home overnight without the parent or caretaker knowing or attempting to determine the child's whereabouts.

- *Other physical neglect*—includes inadequate nutrition, clothing, or hygiene; conspicuous inattention to avoidable hazards in the home; and other forms of reckless disregard of the child's safety and welfare (e.g., driving with the child while intoxicated, leaving a young child in a car unattended).

Educational Neglect

- *Permitted chronic truancy*—habitual absenteeism from school averaging at least 5 days a month if the parent or guardian is informed of the problem and does not attempt to intervene.

- *Failure to enroll or other truancy*—failure to register or enroll a child of mandatory school age, causing the child to miss at least 1 month of school; or a pattern of keeping a school-aged child home without valid reasons.

- *Inattention to special education need*—refusal to allow or failure to obtain recommended remedial education services or neglect in obtaining or following through with treatment for a child's diagnosed learning disorder or other special education need without reasonable cause.

Emotional Neglect

- *Inadequate nurturing or affection*—marked inattention to the child's needs for affection, emotional support, or attention.

- *Chronic or extreme spouse abuse*—exposure to chronic or extreme spouse abuse or other domestic violence in the child's presence.

- *Permitted drug or alcohol abuse*—encouragement or permitting of drug or alcohol use by the child.

- *Permitted other maladaptive behavior*—encouragement or permitting of other maladaptive behavior (e.g., chronic delinquency, severe assault) under circumstances where the parent or caregiver has reason to be aware of the existence and seriousness of the problem but does not intervene.

- *Refusal of psychological care*—refusal to allow needed and available treatment for a child's emotional or behavioral impairment or problem in accordance with a competent professional recommendation.

- *Delay in psychological care*—failure to seek or provide

needed treatment for a child's emotional or behavioral impairment or problem that any reasonable layman would have recognized as needing professional, psychological attention (e.g., suicide attempt).

Psychological Maltreatment or Emotional Abuse

Psychological maltreatment—also known as emotional abuse and neglect—refers to "a repeated pattern of caregiver behavior or extreme incident(s) that convey to children that they are worthless, flawed, unloved, unwanted, endangered, or only of value in meeting another's needs" [according to Stuart N. Hart and Marla Brassard in *Psychosocial Evaluation of Suspected Psychological Maltreatment in Children and Adolescents* (1995)]. Summarizing research and expert opinion, [Hart and Brassard] present six categories of psychological maltreatment:

- Spurning (e.g., belittling, hostile rejecting, ridiculing);

- Terrorizing (e.g., threatening violence against a child, placing a child in a recognizably dangerous situation);

- Isolating (e.g., confining the child, placing unreasonable limitations on the child's freedom of movement, restricting the child from social interactions);

- Exploiting or corrupting (e.g., modeling antisocial behavior such as criminal activities, encouraging prostitution, permitting substance abuse);

- Denying emotional responsiveness (e.g., ignoring the child's attempts to interact, failing to express affection);

- Mental health, medical, and educational neglect (e.g., refusing to allow or failing to provide treatment for serious mental health or medical problems, ignoring the need for services for serious educational needs).

To warrant intervention, psychological maltreatment must be sustained and repetitive. For less severe acts, such as habitual scapegoating or belittling, demonstrable harm to the child is often required for CPS to intervene.

Psychological maltreatment is the most difficult form of child maltreatment to identify. In part, the difficulty in detection occurs because the effects of psychological maltreatment, such as lags in development, learning problems, and speech disorders, are often evident in both children who have experienced and those who have *not* experienced maltreatment. Additionally, the effects of psychological maltreatment may only become evident in later developmental stages of the child's life.

Although any of the forms of child maltreatment may be found alone, they often occur in combination. Psychological maltreatment is almost always present when other forms are identified.

The Prevalence of Child Abuse

U.S. Department of Health and Human Services

Every year, the U.S. Department of Health and Human Services (HHS) publishes the data collected on child abuse by the National Child Abuse and Neglect Data System (NCANDS). The following data was printed in the 2003 edition of the HHS report. According to HHS findings, an estimated 906,000 children were victims of abuse or neglect out of 2.9 million allegations of abuse referred to Child Protective Services (CPS) agencies in 2003. The excerpt of the report that follows provides demographic data on the kinds of abuse reported, and on the age, gender, and ethnicities of the children who were victims of abuse. While the HHS report provides a useful reference for case workers, national polls such as the Gallup Poll, along with surveys of educators and health providers, suggest that the prevalence of child abuse in the United States is likely even greater than the CPS account found in the HHS report.

Child protective services (CPS) agencies respond to the needs of children who are alleged to have been maltreated and ensure that they remain safe. The rate of children who received a disposition by CPS agencies was 45.9 per 1,000 children in the national population. This yields an estimate of 3,353,000 children who received investigations or assessments during 2003.

An estimated 906,000 children were found to be victims, which was approximately 31.7 percent of all children who received an investigation or assessment. A child was counted each time he or she was found to be a victim of maltreatment. The national rate of victimization was 12.4 per 1,000 children. . . .

U.S. Department of Health and Human Services, Administration on Children, Youth and Families, *Child Maltreatment 2003*. Washington, DC: U.S. Government Printing Office, 2005.

The rate of all children who received an investigation or assessment increased from 36.1 per 1,000 children in 1990 to 45.9 per 1,000 children in 2003, which is a 27.1 percent increase. The rate of victimization decreased from 13.4 per 1,000 children in 1990 to 12.4 per 1,000 children in 2003, which is a 7.5 percent decrease.

Patterns of Maltreatment

During 2003, 60.9 percent of victims experienced neglect, 18.9 percent were physically abused, 9.9 percent were sexually abused, 4.9 percent were emotionally or psychologically maltreated, and 2.3 percent were medically neglected. In addition, 16.9 percent of victims experienced such "other" types of maltreatment as "abandonment," "threats of harm to the child," and "congenital drug addiction." States may code any maltreatment type that does not fall into one of the main categories—physical abuse, neglect, medical neglect, sexual abuse, and psychological or emotional maltreatment—as "other." These maltreatment type percentages total more than 100 percent because children who were victims of more than one type of maltreatment were counted for each maltreatment. . . .

There are distinct patterns of maltreatment associated with different reporters of certain types of maltreatment. More than 40 percent of physical abuse victims were reported to CPS by either educational personnel (21.8%) or legal and justice personnel (21.5%). Legal and justice personnel (including law enforcement, correctional facility staff, and court staff) reported 25.7 percent of neglect victims, 25.6 percent of sexual abuse victims, and 29.9 percent of psychological maltreatment victims. Medical personnel reported 26.4 percent of medical neglect victims.

Sex and Age of Victims

For 2003, 48.3 percent of child victims were boys, and 51.7 percent of the victims were girls. The youngest children had the highest rate of victimization. The rate of child victimization of the age group of birth to 3 years was 16.4 per 1,000 children of the same age group. The victimization rate of children in the age group of 4–7 years was 13.8 per 1,000 children in the same age group. Overall, the rate of victimization was inversely related to the age of the child.

The youngest children accounted for the largest percentage of victims. Children younger than 1-year-old accounted for 9.8 percent of victims.

Race and Ethnicity of Victims

Pacific Islander children, American Indian or Alaska Native children, and African-American children had the highest rates of victimization at 21.4, 21.3, and 20.4 per 1,000 children of the same race or ethnicity, respectively. White children and Hispanic children had rates of approximately 11.0 and 9.9 per 1,000 children of the same race or ethnicity, respectively. Asian children had the lowest rate of 2.7 per 1,000 children of the same race or ethnicity.

One-half of all victims were White (53.6%); one-quarter (25.5%) were African-American; and one-tenth (11.5%) were Hispanic. For most racial categories, the largest percentage of victims suffered from neglect.

Disabled Children

Child victims who were reported with a disability accounted for 6.5 percent of all victims in the 34 States that reported these data. Children with the following risk factors were considered as having a disability: mental retardation, emotional disturbance, visual impairment, learning disability, physical disability, behavioral problems, or another medical problem. In general, children with such conditions are undercounted as not every child receives a clinical diagnostic assessment by CPS.

Parents Are Most Likely Perpetrators

More than 80 percent (83.9%) of victims were abused by at least one parent. Approximately two-fifths (40.8%) of child victims were maltreated by their mothers acting alone; another 18.8 percent were maltreated by their fathers acting alone; 16.9 percent were abused by both parents. Victims abused by nonparental perpetrators accounted for 13.4 percent of the total. . . .

Risk Factors for Maltreatment

Some child characteristics or circumstances place children at greater risk for being identified as victims [of maltreatment by the CPS agency] during the investigation process: . . .

- Children who have been identified as victims in the past were 60 percent more likely to be determined to be maltreated compared to children who were not victimized previously.

- Children with allegations of multiple types of maltreatment were 203 percent more likely to be determined to be maltreated than were children with allegations of physical abuse. Children with allegations of sexual abuse were about 48 percent more likely to be considered victims than children with allegations of physical abuse.

- . . . Children who were younger than 4 years old were most likely to be determined to be maltreated compared to all other age groups.

- American Indian or Alaska Native children were 29 percent more likely to be determined victims than White children. This result indicates that even though fewer children of American Indian or Alaska Native descent were determined to be maltreated, of those who were reported, a high percentage were determined to be maltreated.

- Children who were reported by educational personnel were 131 percent more likely to be determined to be maltreated as children reported by social services and mental health personnel. . . .

For many children who experience repeat maltreatment, the efforts of the CPS system have not been successful in preventing subsequent victimization. . . . In this analysis, recurrence is defined as a second substantiated or indicated maltreatment occurring within a 6-month period (183 days). The major results of the analysis are summarized below.

- Child victims who were reported with a disability were 51 percent more likely to experience recurrence than children without a disability.

- In comparison to children who experienced physical abuse, children who were neglected were 31 percent more likely to experience recurrence.

- Children who received postinvestigation services were 20 percent more likely to be found to be maltreated again compared to children who did not.

- Children who had been removed from their home were 15 percent more likely to experience abuse and neglect again than children who remained with their families.

- The youngest children (from birth through age 3) were the most likely to experience a recurrence of maltreatment.

- Compared to White children, Asian-Pacific Islanders were 33 percent less likely to experience recurrence. African-American children were 22 percent less likely to experience recurrence than White children.

- Children reported by "other" or unknown sources, which for the most part were nonprofessionals, were 29 percent more likely to experience recurrence than children reported by social services or mental health personnel. Children reported by educational personnel were 25 percent more likely to experience abuse or neglect again than children reported by social services or mental health personnel.

- Children for whom the perpetrator was not a parent were 21 percent less likely to experience recurrence than children who were abused by their mother.

Child Sexual Abuse Is Occurring Within the Catholic Church

Boston Globe

Starting in June 2001, when Cardinal Bernard Law, the archbishop of Boston at the time, disclosed that he had promoted Father John Geoghan despite recent accusations that Geoghan had allegedly molested seven boys, the investigative staff of the Boston Globe *set out to determine whether Geoghan's case was an anomaly or part of a larger pattern. Over the next four months, the* Globe *ran nearly three hundred stories about sexual abuse by priests and, as a result of the* Globe's *reportage, 176 priests in the United States were pulled from their assignments. After the incident came to light, the Catholic Church began taking an active hand in disclosing the scope of the problem. Church surveys from 2005 report that at least 5,148 clergy were accused of abusing at least 11,750 victims between 1950 and the end of 2004.*

In the following excerpt from the book Betrayal: The Crisis in the Catholic Church, *the* Boston Globe *documents the promotion of Fathers Joseph Birmingham and Paul Shanley within the Catholic Church throughout the 1960s and 1970s despite accusations of abuse and the Catholic leadership's initial response, or lack thereof, to victims' complaints. Although Birmingham died in 1989, before the scandal broke, Shanley and Geoghan were eventually convicted of multiple counts of child rape. Geoghan was later murdered in prison. Cardinal Law has since been awarded an important ceremonial position in Rome.*

The investigative staff of the Boston Globe *consists of Matt Carroll, Kevin Cullen, Thomas Farragher, Stephen Kurkijian, Michael Paulson, Sacha Pfeiffer, Michael Rezendes, and Walter V. Robinson.*

The Investigative Staff of the *Boston Globe, Betrayal: The Crisis in the Catholic Church.* New York: Little, Brown and Company, 2002. Copyright © 2002 by the *Boston Globe.* Reproduced by permission of Little, Brown and Co., Inc.

Why some priests, and why some men in general, are sexually attracted to minors remains a much-debated and highly controversial issue, one cluttered with unanswered questions. But while the origins of the crisis remain uncertain, the reality that numerous priests have become abusers is not.

[Since 1987], an estimated fifteen hundred American priests have faced allegation of sexual abuse, according to Jason Berry, the reporter who documented Gilbert Gauthé's abuses and the author of *Lead Us Not into Temptation: Catholic Priests and the Sexual Abuse of Children* [(2000)], in an authoritative early examination of the issue. In the aftermath of the [Father John] Geoghan disclosures in January 2002, the names of more than ninety priests alleged to have sexually abused minors were turned over to Massachusetts law enforcement officials by the Boston archdiocese alone. And eleven sitting priests were abruptly removed from their posts—eight of them after Church officials discovered credible allegations of sexual abuse in their files—even though Cardinal [Bernard] Law [of the Boston archdiocese] had publicly asserted weeks before that all such priests had been removed from their assignments. The other three were removed when new victims came forward for the first time. Law's decision to cooperate with prosecutors, made under pressure, spurred Church officials in other major American cities, including Philadelphia, Los Angeles, and New York, to share with authorities the names of allegedly abusive priests in their dioceses as well. As a result of reverberations from the Boston scandal, more than one hundred and seventy priests suspected of molesting minors had either resigned or been taken off duty in the early months of 2002, according to a nationwide survey of Catholic dioceses by the Associated Press.

For every name passed along to prosecutors, a secret Church file of some type existed in virtually every case. But the smattering of information released by dioceses across the nation underscored an alarming reality: repeat abusers such as

Geoghan, [James] Porter, [Rudy] Kos, and Gauthé, all of whom were convicted for their crimes, appear not to have been the aberrations some Church officials claimed they were. Serial molesters "are not as much of an anomaly as people would like to think," said A.W. Richard Sipe, a former priest and psychotherapist who specialized in treating priests who abuse children. The Geoghans and Porters of the priesthood, he said, are "extreme examples, in a way, because they're the ones who have gotten the notoriety. But there are many priests who have just never been reported."

Reports of Abuse Fall on Deaf Ears

In the case of . . . Joseph E. Birmingham, the abuses were reported, but the reports fell on deaf ears. Like Geoghan, Birmingham served as a priest for nearly three decades, from his ordination in 1960 until his death in 1989 at age fifty-five. Like Geoghan, he was rotated through six parishes, despite a string of complaints about his sexual compulsion. Like Geoghan, he allegedly accumulated dozens of victims even though high Church officials knew he was molesting children. And, like Geoghan, the number of Birmingham's alleged victims is large—as many as twenty-five alone from his third assignment at St. Michael's parish in Lowell, north of Boston, in the 1970s. But in Birmingham's case, the public evidence that the Church stood by and did nothing to stop him early in his career appears to be even stronger. . . .

Howard McCabe himself at first doubted his son [Michael's] innocent admission and intended to follow the advice of a neighbor and keep the information secret. But he changed his mind when Michael told him that a grade school friend, Peter Taylor, had also been molested by Birmingham, and Taylor's father, Frank, confirmed that his son had indeed been victimized. Once the shock wore off and the anger took hold, the men acted.

"He came pounding on my door, and he had fire in his eyes," Howard McCabe said, recalling the sight from almost four decades ago of Frank Taylor quaking with anger on his front porch. "He was a big man, but an awful gentle man, and he wanted to kill Birmingham."

Stunned and chagrined, the two men contacted their local pastor, who arranged for them and their sons to meet with Church administrators at archdiocesan headquarters in Boston. . . .

"I was scared to death," recalled Peter Taylor. "I was just a kid."

With Birmingham present, the two boys were ordered to repeat their complaints, in detail. Once they had described to the adults at the table what had happened to them, it was Birmingham's turn to speak.

He denied any wrongdoing.

"It was wicked embarrassing for a kid to have to tell this story in public," Michael McCabe said. "I couldn't believe they were making us do that, making us say this in front of him and making us look like liars. When we left I said to my dad, 'I told the truth, Dad. I really did.'"

The arduous experience seemed to have been worthwhile. Later the same day, their pastor paid a visit to the Taylor family's home, where the two men and their sons had gathered after the meeting. He had good news to relay: Birmingham, the pastor said, would be removed from Sudbury and sent to Salem, north of Boston, where he would be made chaplain of Salem Hospital and receive psychiatric treatment.

Transferred to a New Parish, the Priest Offends Again

True to the pastor's word, Birmingham was transferred to Salem in 1964. Pleased and relieved, Howard McCabe felt his decision to notify the Church of the boys' complaints had been the correct one. But that case of relief evaporated about a year later, when his son saw Birmingham skiing in New Hampshire with a busload of young boys on what appeared to be an official school outing. The thought that their complaints had been brushed aside by Church authorities was crushing to the men's faith. "It was devastating," Howard McCabe said.

"I left the Church," said Frank Taylor, now seventy-seven. "I never went back again." . . .

Over the course of the priest's career, at least seven people from at least two different parishes notified Boston archdiocesan officials of his alleged abuse. In his second assignment, a group of five Salem mothers also visited the chancery, in about 1970, to complain that Birmingham had molested several of their children, sometimes during confession. Their pleas too went unheeded. . . . They wanted to ensure that Birmingham's new pastor in Lowell would be notified of his history and that Birmingham would receive psychiatric care.

Until several of their sons told them that Birmingham had molested them, the women had believed that the priest's move to Lowell had been a routine transfer; they had even held a farewell party for him. But during their chancery meeting with Monsignor John Jennings, "We got no place," said [Mary] McGee [one of the mothers]. "He was sitting there, pompous, and pacifying us. At the end of the meeting he said, 'You know, ladies, you have to be very careful of slander.'"

Distraught, McGee paid a visit to Rev. John B. McCormack, who was then serving as regional director of Catholic Charities in Salem, and who later became bishop of Manchester, New Hampshire. McCormack acknowledges that parents complained to him that Birmingham was molesting children and says he referred them to "the pastor of the parish who was responsible for Father Birmingham's ministry." But Birmingham remained a priest in Lowell and continued to victimize young boys such as David Lyko, who says he was fondled by Birmingham about a dozen times when he was nine or ten, and Olan Horne who said he received a beating

Defrocked Catholic priest Paul Shanley is led out of the courtroom in February 2005, after being sentenced to twelve to fifteen years in prison for raping a child. © Charles Krupa/ Pool/Reuters/CORBIS

from Birmingham when he was fourteen or fifteen after resisting his advances.

Three Decades' Worth of Abuse

In the spring of 2002, within weeks after Birmingham's abuse was revealed in Boston newspapers, more than forty of his alleged victims had come forward.

In March a former Salem man, James Hogan, filed a lawsuit against the Boston archdiocese and New Hampshire Bishop McCormack, alleging that in the 1960s McCormack—who was assigned to St. James's in Salem at the same time Birmingham was—saw Birmingham taking him to his rectory bedroom and did nothing to stop it. That lawsuit was later amended to include an additional thirty-nine alleged victims. McCormack has acknowledged that in about 1970 he was warned that Birmingham was molesting children. But he has denied that he ever saw Birmingham take boys into his rectory bedroom. Separately, Thomas Blanchette, formerly of Sudbury, alleged that Birmingham molested him and his four brothers—attacks that included attempted rape—at Our Lady of Fatima in the 1960s. And Paul Cultrera, a former altar boy who says Birmingham began molesting him in Salem when he was a high school freshman in 1963 or 1964, disclosed publicly that he had received a $60,000 settlement from the archdiocese in 1996. . . .

The total number of children Birmingham abused is unknown. But during his three decades as a priest, Birmingham made a grand tour of parishes in the Boston archdiocese. After serving in Sudbury, Salem, and Lowell, he had yet another assignment at St. Columbkille's in Brighton—where he established a youth drop-in center—before he was promoted to pastor of St. Ann's in Gloucester in 1985. His last assignment before his death was at St. Brigid's in Lexington. He also served as juvenile-court chaplain at Brighton Municipal Court, and he frequently took teenage parishioners on out-of-state field trips; in his suit, Hogan alleges that Birmingham abused him during ski trips to Vermont and an eighth-grade trip to Arizona, Nevada, and California.

"What I know now is that I should have gone to the police," said McGee. "But I thought I'd go to the Church and I thought the Church would take care of it." . . .

An Unconventional Priest Works with Troubled Youth

While the 1960s were an era of massive social upheaval for American society, they also marked a time of radical change for the Roman Catholic Church and its priesthood. And in Boston, no priest embodied that change more than Rev. Paul R. Shanley. . . .

In 1960, when he left St. John's Seminary as a newly ordained priest, Shanley sported a youthful, clean-cut look. Photos taken around the time of his ordination show an attractive, freshly shorn young man with a broad, easy smile. But within a few years, he had cultivated a far different image, one that mirrored the counterculture sensibility of the time. He grew his brown hair long, until it fell below his Roman collar, and wore bushy sideburns that snaked partway down his cheeks. Eventually, he stopped wearing his collar altogether, trading his traditional priestly attire for plaid shirts and blue jeans.

It wasn't only Shanley's unconventional dress and shaggy hairstyle that made him stand out. In the midst of the tumult of the decade in which he was ordained, Shanley frequently challenged Church teachings, particularly its condemnation of homosexuality, and clashed vocally and publicly with his superiors, including Cardinal [Humberto S.] Medeiros.

Shanley openly embraced ostracized minorities such as gays, lesbians, and transsexuals, and in the early 1970s created his "ministry to alienated youth" for runaways, drug abusers, drifters, and teenagers struggling with their sexual identity. His unique, unprecedented ministry earned him the unofficial titles of "street priest" and "hippie priest." His outspokenness won him hero status among many of Boston's alienated young people and placed him in frequent conflict with his superiors.

A Sexual Predator

It was also what Shanley said in private that set him apart. And it was what he did behind closed doors that, four decades after his ordination, brought him far more notoriety than did his rebellious dress and preaching style.

In the parishes and counseling rooms where desperate and troubled young people sought his help, Shanley was a sexual predator, a skilled manipulator who used his power and authority to prey on those who came to him for guidance and support. Therapy sessions became the settings for molestation and rape.

The Boston archdiocese has paid at least five settlements to Shanley's victims, including a $40,000 payment in about 1993 to a man who notified Church officials that he had repeatedly been anally raped by Shanley around 1972, when he was twelve or thirteen. Another man received a $100,000 settlement in 1998 after reporting a four-year sexual relationship with Shanley that began in 1965, when he was in the fifth grade.

But the breadth of Shanley's criminal behavior, and the extent to which he was coddled and protected by top Church officials, remained hidden until a lawsuit filed in February 2002 by Gregory Ford—who alleges he was repeatedly raped by Shanley in the 1980s—forced the release of the archdiocese's confidential files on the priest. More than sixteen hundred pages of previously secret Church records made clear that, for more than a decade, Law and his deputies paid no heed to detailed 1967 allegations of misconduct against Shanley and reacted casually to repeated complaints that he had publicly endorsed sexual relations between men and boys.

The Church Defends the Troubled Priest

Law and his subordinates were so unconcerned about Shanley's behavior that, in 1988, two decades after the detailed complaints about his aberrant behavior began to trickle into the archdiocese, an accusation that Shanley had initiated a sexually explicit conversation was ignored. . . . Yet despite evidence in the chancery's files about the 1967 accusations and Shanley's bizarre sexual views, Law's deputy Bishop Robert Banks concluded in a memo that nothing could be done because Shanley denied that the incident occurred.

The Shanley record reveals Medeiros as similarly complicit. At a talk in Rochester, New York, in 1977, Shanley publicly asserted that he could think of no sexual act that caused "psychic" damage to children, including incest and bestiality, and argued that the child is often the seducer in man-boy sexual relationships. In a letter to Medeiros written shortly after that talk, an appalled New York Catholic vented her dismay at Shanley's remarks. No apparent action was taken.

Shanley's public advocacy of homosexuality eventually attracted the attention of Vatican officials, one of whom wrote to Medeiros requesting an explanation. In his February 1979 reply to Cardinal Franjo Seper in Rome, Medeiros called Shanley "a troubled priest." Two months later, Medeiros was alerted by a New York City lawyer that Shanley had been quoted making similar remarks in an interview about man-boy love with a publication called *Gaysweek*. The only action taken by Church officials was to remove Shanley from his street ministry and send him to a suburban parish [in Newton, Massachusetts]. . . .

Priest's Career Continues to Flourish

In Newton Shanley's career flourished. Despite his troubled track record, he was promoted to pastor six years later by Cardinal Law, then the newly arrived archbishop, in 1985. Four months after that, the archdiocese reacted nonchalantly when a woman alerted the chancery that Shanley gave another talk in Rochester in which he once again endorsed sexual relations between men and boys. In response to the second Rochester letter, Rev. McCormack wrote a friendly note to Shanley, a seminary classmate. In a letter signed "Fraternally in Christ" and containing little sense of urgency, McCormack wrote: "Would you care to comment on the remarks she made? You can either put them in writing or we could get together some day about it." The files contained no evidence that Shanley responded to the request.

The Shanley file also revealed that top Church officials had evidence of the priest's abusive behavior at least as early as the late 1960s. In one handwritten letter, a priest at the Shrine of Our Lady of La Salette in Attleboro, near the Rhode Island border, notified the archdiocese that a young boy had told him that Shanley had masturbated him at a cabin in the Blue Hills, a woodland reservation south of Boston. The letter reported that Shanley routinely brought teenagers to the cabin on weekends, and it provided names, telephone numbers, and addresses of other possible young victims. Church files contain no hint that the allegations were ever investigated. But with an arrogance that defined his persona, Shanley denied the charges in defiant letters in which he offered sarcastic assessments of his accusers and referred to his own "brilliance." In another letter, Shanley used a contemptuous adage to refer to a woman who had accused him of molesting a boy: "Put a Roman collar on a lamp-post and some woman will fall in love with it."

Shanley's diaries and occasional newsletters, undated but also in his files, showed that he contracted venereal disease and instructed teenagers on how to inject drugs. Yet despite Shanley's damning case file, Law gave him a glowing tribute when the priest retired in 1996. In a February 29 letter the cardinal declared, "Without doubt over all of these years of generous and zealous care, the lives and hearts of many people have been touched by your sharing of the Lord's Spirit. You are truly appreciated for all that you have done."

A Long History of Sexual Abuse

The total number of Shanley's victims may never be known, but his involvement with children predated his years as a priest. Before his first parish assignment at St. Patrick's Church in Stoneham, north of Boston, Shanley worked with retarded children, orphans, juvenile delinquents, and poor and black youngsters at numerous organizations in Massachusetts and New Hampshire, including Camp Fatima, the Cardinal's Home for Children, St. Francis Boys Home, the Catholic Boys Guidance Center, the Dorchester Settlement House, and Camp Dorchester. In Stoneham Shanley began a Friday night "Top Ten Club" for local youth at the town hall, which he transformed for the occasion into a disco with live music and psychedelic lighting. In Braintree, he ran teen folk masses that attracted scores of young people. He established a retreat house for youth workers on a ninety-five-acre farm in Weston, Vermont, and named it "Rivendell" after the idyllic valley in J.R.R. Tolkien's *The Hobbit*. He also served as chaplain at Boston State College and held appointments at Warwick House in Roxbury and Exodus Center in Milton, just south of Boston. Both involved close work with teenagers. From all those periods, victims have now come forward. . . .

After leaving Newton in 1990 for a "sabbatical" in California, Shanley was placed on paid sick leave and surfaced at St. Anne's parish in San Bernardino, his way paved by a letter from Bishop Banks asserting that Shanley was a priest in good standing in Boston. Shanley occasionally worked on weekends at St. Anne's and—unbeknownst to his colleagues there—spent his weekdays running the Cabana Club, a "clothing optional" gay motel in nearby Palm Springs, with another Boston priest who was then also on sick leave in California, Rev. John J. White. Shanley and White co-owned the property, even as they were receiving monthly payments from the Boston archdiocese.

In the mid-1990s, with the consent of the Boston archdiocese, Shanley was acting director of Leo House, the Church-run guest house in New York. As recently as 1997—after the Boston archdiocese had already paid monetary settlements to several of Shanley's victims—Law did not object to Shanley's application to be director of the facility. Church files contain a draft of a letter written by Law recommending Shanley for the director's position, although New York Cardinal John O'Connor vetoed the idea and the letter was never sent. So Shanley returned to California, where he worked as a "senior civilian volunteer" for the San Diego Police Department.

Speaking in 1969 about the dangers that face runaways and street kids, Shanley seemed to dare the reporter interviewing him to scratch below the surface of his ministry.

"Whom do you want to get these kids first? Professional counselors or the hustlers and the psychotics who prey on young people?" he asked. In the same interview, Shanley described the teenagers he worked with as "victims of violence, of disease, sexual deviates, and drugs."

Too Many Victims to Count

Nearly thirty-five years after a sex abuse complaint was first made against him, Shanley finally attracted the attention of police. In early May of 2002, as many of his alleged victims came forward for the first time in the wake of newspaper accounts of his abusive past, Shanley was arrested in San Diego and pleaded not guilty to three counts of child rape dating to the 1980s. The charges were filed on behalf of Paul Busa, a former Newton man who alleged that Shanley abused him from 1983 to 1990, beginning when he was six. The seventy-one-year-old priest faced the prospect of spending the rest of his life in prison. . . .

One of the most striking aspects of the wave of clergy sex abuse complaints triggered by the revelations in Boston was this: the allegations knew no geographic bounds. It would have been troubling enough if the abuse had been limited to New England. But around the country, there had been other Shanleys, other Birminghams. . . . From Maine to Florida to Los Angeles, new victims came forward to tell their stories, emboldened by other victims who had come forward before them. . . .

As long as dioceses across the country continued to keep abuse complaints confidential, the true number of abusive priests would remain unknown. Absent a policy of openness by Church officials from small-town parishes to the Vatican, the public was left to wonder whether the explosion of publicity about sexually deviant priests centered around a small minority of clergymen or only scraped at the surface of a much larger problem. Meanwhile, another issue loomed: how many victims were out there, scared, silent, and ashamed?

Church Sexual Abuse Mirrors Abuse in American Society

Stephen J. Rossetti

Although the sexual abuse of children—mainly boys—by Catholic priests is a serious problem, argues Stephen J. Rossetti, an overly simplistic understanding of the problem makes it more difficult to address the underlying issues and protect children. Drawing upon his experience as a psychologist as well as a priest, Rossetti argues that most child molesters are not pedophiles, or adults who are sexually attracted to children, and therefore most can be helped. He contends that priests as a population are no more likely to be child molesters than the general population, that celibate priests are not more likely to be homosexuals than the rest of the population, and that homosexuals do not molest children more than the general population. To protect children and address the problem of priests exploiting children, Rossetti recommends that the leadership of the Catholic Church communicate openly with the larger community, and he argues that it is better to counsel and closely supervise offending priests than to unreservedly defrock them. Stephen J. Rossetti is the president of the St. Luke Institute, a therapeutic facility in Maryland for priests who have sexually offended. He has served as a consultant to the U.S. Conference of Catholic Bishops' ad hoc committee on child sexual abuse.

When complex situations are given simplistic understandings and simplistic solutions, people will inevitably be hurt. The phenomenon of child sexual abuse, in the priesthood and in society at large, is a complex issue that does not admit of simple understandings or simple solutions. It is important that we examine the issue in greater depth; otherwise the church and society will not only repeat past mistakes but also make new mistakes in response. Most important, without a more informed understanding and a more reasoned response, children will be no safer and may, inadvertently, be placed at even greater risk.

I would like to discuss five major oversimplifications and distortions regarding child sexual abuse. . . .

Sex Offenders Can Be Rehabilitated

1. All child molesters are pedophiles and all pedophiles are incurable. They are dangerous men who abuse scores of minors. There is no hope for them. As with all distortions, there is some truth to these statements. There are child molesters who are pedophiles, that is, they are sexually attracted to *pre*pubescent minors, and some molest scores of minors. These high-profile, notorious abusers, who capture public attention, are usually resistant to psychological treatment. One does not speak of trying to change or "cure" their sexual attraction to minors. While some pedophiles can be helped to control their sexual desires, many cannot. Since these persons pose an ongoing threat to society, after serving an appropriate prison term, they ought to live in a kind of lifelong parole setting with absolutely no unsupervised contact with minors.

Fortunately, real pedophiles are the exception among adults who sexually abuse minors. Most abusers are not pedophiles. Most abuse *post*-pubescent minors and, all things being equal, are much more amenable to treatment. While both pedophiles and those who molest post-pubescent minors have committed a heinous crime, it would be an error to apply exactly the same remedy to them all. With treatment and supervision, many adults who molest adolescents can go on to live productive lives. But prudence would still dictate that these adults should be supervised whenever interacting with adolescents.

John Geoghan, for example, a former priest of the Archdiocese of Boston, reportedly molested over 100 children. He went through several treatment regimens, apparently to no avail. He is now in prison and will remain there for many years.[1] On the other hand, most perpetrators of child sexual abuse are members or friends of the victims' own families, such as fathers, stepfathers, uncles, cousins or neighbors. Would we treat a father who molests his daughter in exactly the same fashion as we would a pedophile like John Geoghan? Indeed, both should be subjected to the law and ought to pay for their crimes. But the ability to rehabilitate the incestuous father is much better than the habituated pedophile. We would be better served if the father could be eventually returned to society, with appropriate safeguards.

Fred Berlin, M.D., an international expert on the treatment of child abusers, reported a relapse rate of only 2.9 percent over a five- to six-year period among 173 lay abusers who were treatment-compliant. Similarly, a church-run facility recently followed for one to five years after treatment 121 priests who sexually molested post-pubescent minors. Of those who finished an intensive treatment program and continued in follow-up care, only three relapsed—2.5 percent. While we grieve for those who were molested by these offenders who relapsed, treatment and supervision probably saved many other children from being molested.

It is often suggested in the public forum that offenders molest scores of victims and that there is an enormously high rate of relapse. But such high statistics are taken from clinical studies using forensic populations, which is a more disturbed and dysfunctional sample. If we are serious about protecting children, it is time for the public and the psychologists they quote to use more up-to-date and sophisticated clinical data. A father who molests his daughter and a compulsive pedophile are very different in their clinical profiles. To fashion a proper response that is likely to be effective, society needs to understand the complex differences and develop appropriate

1. John Geoghan was murdered in prison in 2003.

responses. In the end, child safety depends upon it. Moreover, it is important to note that most priests who sexually molest minors are clinically more like the abusive father than the compulsive pedophile. John Geoghan is the rare exception, thank God.

Priests Are Not More Likely than the Public to Abuse Children

2. Priests are more likely to be child molesters than others because they are celibate. Celibacy distorts one's sexuality, and a celibate priesthood attracts a larger proportion of men with sexual problems. The first half of this simplification has been largely discredited in recent media stories. Researchers and clinicians have generally accepted the fact that celibacy does not cause child sexual abuse. In fact, the sexual difficulties and inner psychological problems that give rise to child sexual abuse are largely in place long before a person enters into the formation process for a celibate priesthood. In addition, most adults who sexually molest minors are, or will be, married.

The second half of the statement, "a celibate priesthood attracts a larger proportion of men with sexual problems," is currently being debated. Some have said that we seem to have so many child molesters in the priesthood because celibacy attracts people with sexual problems. Is that true?

It is a complex problem that demands a complex answer. Some people with sexual problems seek out a celibate lifestyle in an unconscious attempt to escape their own sexuality. I know this for a fact because I have counseled some who admit the same. Nonetheless, it is dangerous to summarize from the particular to the general.

By analogy, one might say that it is likely that there are some people who enter the police force because of their own distorted needs for power, authority and violence. But I suspect the mayor and police chief would have some strong words for anyone who tried to suggest that the police force in general is power-hungry, controlling and violent. It is a logical fallacy to generalize based on particular cases.

This brings to light the basic assumption that underlies these distortions—namely, that priests are more likely to be child abusers than others in society. Is that true? The short answer is: we do not know. There are simply no prevalence rates of perpetration of child sexual abuse either in society at large or in the priesthood. The reason for the lack of data is inherent in the crime. It is very difficult to gather a sample of adult males and ask them if they have ever sexually abused a minor. Even if they told the truth, gathering such data would present thorny ethical and legal considerations.

Only a Small Fraction of Priests Abuse Children

The best the church can do to estimate the prevalence rate of sexual abuse of minors by priests is to count the number of priests who have "substantial" allegations of child sexual abuse against them and compare this number with the total number of priests.

When the Archdiocese of Boston reportedly released the names of 80 priests who had sexually molested minors over the last 50 years, people asked, "How can there be so many priests who abuse children? There are only about 800 priests in the archdiocese, so this represents 10 percent of our entire presbyterate!" But the numbers were misleading. On March 15 the official publication of the archdiocese, *The Pilot,* said the number of substantial allegations was approximately 60, and it is important to note that this number represents the total number of accused priests over 50 years. The editorial estimated that there were probably about 3,000 priests who served in the archdiocese during these 50 years, so the ratio is about 2 percent.

Similarly, the Archdiocese of Philadelphia recently went over its records since 1950. There were 2,154 priests who served during this time frame, and there were "credible allegations" against 35. This is about 1.6 percent. Likewise, the Archdiocese of Chicago reviewed its records. In the past 40 years, out of 2,200 priests who served, about 40, or 1.8 percent, had received credible allegations of abuse.

While one case is one too many, especially when perpetrated by a man with a sacred trust—a Catholic priest—the suggestion that priests are more likely to be child abusers than other males has yet to be established. In fact, the early statistics challenge that assumption and actually imply that the number of priests who molest could be lower. It would be reasonable to believe that the number of adult males who molest minors in society is at least as large. One need only speak with the dedicated and overworked social workers who staff our child protective services around the country to know that the percentage of adult males who molest minors is not insignificant. I conducted a survey of 1,810 adults in the United States and Canada and found that over 19 percent of them had been the victims of sexual molestation by an adult before the age of 18. This suggests that there are many perpetrators of child sexual abuse in our society. While we are shocked, and rightly so, that there would be 60 priests in the Archdiocese of Boston who have molested minors, we should be equally shocked at just how common child sexual abuse is throughout our society.

Homosexuals Are No More Likely to Abuse Children than Anyone Else

3. We have so many child abusers in the priesthood because a celibate priesthood attracts homosexuals. No mainstream researcher would suggest that there is any link between homosexuality and true pedophilia, that is, sexual attraction of an adult to prepubescent minors. In addition, most adults in society who sexually molest minors are not homosexually oriented.

The rejoinder to this is the fact that most victims of priests are young males. But this, too, is easily open to misinterpretation. Most priests who molest minors were themselves molested as minors; their sexual abuse of minors is for many of them a kind of re-enactment of their own abuse and may have little to do with their sexual orientation. I have known some heterosexually oriented males who molested young males.

Nonetheless, a significant number of priests who sexually molest minors are involved with post-pubescent adolescent males, about 14 to 17 years of age. It appears to be true that many in this sub-population of priest child-molesters are homosexually oriented. But theirs is a particular kind of homosexuality, which one might call "regressed" or "stunted." These homosexual men are emotionally stuck in adolescence themselves, and so are at risk for being sexually active with teenage males. The issue is therefore not so much homosexuality but rather their stunted emotional development.

The problem is not that the church ordains homosexuals. Rather, it is that the church has ordained regressed or stunted homosexuals. The solution, then, is not to ban all homosexuals from ordained ministry, but rather to screen out regressed homosexuals before ordination. Preparation for ordination should directly assess the seminarian's ability and commitment to live a chaste, celibate life.

We are in a dangerous period that is intensely emotional. Everyone, inside and outside the church, wants to find simplistic solutions. "Getting rid of homosexuals" from the priesthood will not be as successful as some predict in ridding the church of child abusers and in the end may cause even more human damage.

The Church Must Be Transparent and Accountable

4. The U.S. bishops continue to be secretive about child sex abuse cases and fail to follow the law and report these cases to legal authorities. They cannot be trusted. Much of the real energy behind the current furor is anger directed at the Catholic bishops. People feel betrayed. But over the past 10 years I have witnessed bishops tackling scores of cases with great care and solicitude for victims and perpetrators. Yet they are currently being depicted as being grossly negligent. How can we understand this apparent contradiction?

It is true that in a minority of cases, victims have been asked to sign "gag orders." The diocese agrees to settle a civil suit; it pays out a certain sum of money, and it stipulates that the victim will not publicly reveal what happened. In retrospect, this can be recognized as a mistake. While one can understand a bishop's desire not to "scandalize" people and to protect the church's image, such actions promote distrust and allegations of secrecy.

Nevertheless, it is not true that bishops are circumventing the reporting requirements about child sexual abuse. Again, the reality is much more complicated. In most states, child-abuse reporting laws require that suspected incidents be reported only if the victim who comes forward is still a minor. I called one state's child protective services and asked if they would investigate a report if the victim was no longer a minor. The answer was no.

One might then suggest that the bishop report the allegation of abuse to the criminal authorities. There are two problems with this. First of all, the law does not require the bishop to report the allegation if the victim is no longer a minor and the bishop has a concurrent obligation to maintain pastoral confidentiality with those who confide in him, just as a secular counselor would. If the law does not give him "permission" to break confidentiality and report the abuse, then he is obligated to protect confidentiality. Second, even if he did report the allegation of abuse to the criminal authorities, the statute of limitations may well have expired, and there is little hope that the justice system would be of any assistance. Unfortunately, only a minority of cases of child sexual abuse are successfully adjudicated criminally.

The Need for Standard Reporting Practices

Making an analogy with my second profession as a psychologist might be helpful. As a licensed psychologist, I am a mandated reporter of child sexual abuse. If I learn of a case of child sexual abuse, and I know an identified victim who is still a minor, I am obliged to report such cases to child protective services. But if I am counseling a 40-year-old woman, for example, who reveals to me that her uncle abused her 25 years ago, should I report her uncle? In many states, the law does not require this. Most likely the woman would not want it reported. And in a therapeutic setting, I have an ethical and legal obligation to protect this woman's confidentiality and privacy. So since the law does not stipulate that I must break confidentiality to report the abuse, I am obligated by law to maintain her privacy.

The bishops are being excoriated for not reporting cases of abuse. But the laws do not require it in most situations that the church faces. The bishops also have a pastoral obligation to maintain confidentiality. What many dioceses are doing is counseling the victims that they themselves are free to report the incident to civil authorities. In fact, the church should encourage victims to report such an incident. But one can clearly argue that unless the law requires the church to break confidentiality—which the law usually does not do—it is up to the victim to report.

A disturbing trend is now appearing. Legal authorities are demanding from Catholic dioceses a complete list of all past allegations against priests of child sexual abuse. In most cases, these legal authorities are going beyond the requirements of the law. They are setting up a kind of double standard that I believe should be tested in the courts. While church authorities may willingly comply, it is a dangerous precedent to have one standard for priests and another for the rest of society.

What is needed for the protection of children is not a different standard of reporting only for priests, but a better reporting system that sets a better standard for all; this ought to include revisiting the length of the statute of limitations in child sexual abuse cases.

Supervising Offending Priests

5. The safest thing for children is to defrock any priest who is guilty of child sexual abuse. The church has been grossly negligent by continuing to shuffle such priests from parish to parish, where they re-offend. It is true that the Archdiocese of Boston made a grievous error in reassigning John Geoghan to a parish after he became known as a child molester. There was no excuse for such an action. Any priest who sexually molests a minor should never be returned to parish ministry or any ministry involving minors. But I would say clearly that there have been very few cases of such actions in the last decade. Even in Boston, almost all the priests with substantial allegations of child sexual abuse were either retired early, dismissed from ministry or placed in assignments not involving minors. Even in Boston, the case of John Geoghan is an exception, but it is being portrayed as if it were normal in the church.

This raises a more difficult question: should any priest who has a past history of molesting a minor remain in the priesthood? Clearly; the public is saying no. And I think public pressure will have its way. Around the country, priests with a substantial allegation of child molestation are being dismissed from any form of ministry. The damage to the church's credibility is so large, and the legal and financial fallout is so great, that many of our leaders feel forced to expel them all. This is certainly the safest action for the church.

But is this the safest course of action for children? When priests are dismissed from ministry, they go out into society unsupervised and perhaps even untreated. Then they are free to do as they please. If they have been convicted of a sexual crime against minors, they may have to be registered in compliance with various state or local laws. But, as noted previously, there are few criminal convictions against child sex abusers. Either the statute of limitations has run out, or the victim does not want a criminal trial, or there is simply insufficient evidence. Whatever the reason, when the church "defrocks" these priests, they are no longer supervised. One might recall the case of James Porter, who was expelled from the Diocese of Fall River in Massachusetts and returned to life as a layman. He married and was eventually convicted of molesting his children's baby sitter.

The question of what to do with child molesters is complex. Some bishops have been sending priests accused of child sexual abuse for intensive psychotherapeutic treatment and then, depending upon the man's response to treatment, taking the ones who present the least risk and returning them to a limited, supervised ministry that did not involve direct contact with minors. Of the scores of such cases, very, very few have re-offended. The public has been outraged that these men were still in ministry at all. But I believe that time will show that the bishops' actions were both prudent and in the best interests of all in society, especially our children. If all these priests had been summarily dismissed from the priesthood, it is very probable that more children would have been abused. Putting a priest through treatment and leaving him in a limited ministry, such as that of chaplain to a convent or nursing home, is not without some risk. But there is more risk in releasing him into society. . . .

Working Together to Protect Children

People naturally do not like complexity and uncertainty, especially with upsetting realities like the sexual abuse of children. . . . We want child sexual abuse to be the exclusive crime of a few perpetrators who are "out there" and not part of our families. We would like to accuse an identifiable group of deviants who are different from us. We want our lives and the lives of our children to be completely and absolutely free of risk. We want a clear and simple solution, but there is none. Facing the fact that the sexual abuse of children is a crime that not only occurs in the priesthood, but most of the time is perpetrated in our own families, is a most painful truth. Not facing the complexities of child sexual abuse makes our children less safe, and pointing the finger at a few while missing the many ignores the cries of children in our own midst.

It is time for our church and our society, for priests and for families to work together in a new partnership to combat the grave evil that is the sexual abuse of children.

The Internet Can Abet
Child Abuse

Michael McGrath

In the following article, Michael McGrath argues that because the Internet is prevalent in most children's lives and because children's Internet use is largely unsupervised, they are vulnerable to sexual solicitation and other forms of harassment from adult Internet users. After noting various ways in which children have been victimized via the Internet, McGrath offers recommendations on how parents can best protect children from online sexual solicitation, exploitation by online child pornography, and in rare instances, abduction by someone who has befriended them via the Internet.

Michael McGrath is a clinical associate professor of psychiatry at the University of Rochester Medical Center and associate chair for ambulatory services in the Department of Psychiatry and Behavioral Health at Unity Health Systems in Rochester, New York. McGrath specializes in forensic psychiatry and criminal profiling. He is a founding member of the Academy of Behavioral Profiling.

In the United States, nearly every child has access to the Internet at home, at school, at friends' homes, at the local library, at an Internet café, or at all of those places. Security and supervision of children's Internet use vary widely. For instance, Internet access at an elementary or middle school is usually filtered and closely supervised. On the other hand, many public libraries use no filtering and do not supervise Internet use. Many parents are completely naïve regarding the potential dangers to their children posed by the Internet. Parents often have a completely different Internet experience than their children. Parents use the Internet mostly for e-mail, shopping, and research. Children use the Internet to communicate with people using Instant Messaging, chat, and e-mail; participate in interactive games; download music; do their homework; and perform all sorts of other activities. Today children live a large share of their lives in the virtual world. Unfortunately, the increased exposure to inappropriate content and contact with people often leads to children being victimized.

According to a [2000] survey conducted through New Hampshire University between August 1999 and February 2000, of 1,501 youths aged 10 to 17 who regularly use the Internet in the year prior to the survey:

- About one in five received some form of sexual solicitation over the Internet.

- One in thirty-three received an aggressive sexual solicitation (request to meet, talk by phone, etc.).

- One in four was exposed to unwanted pictures of nudity or sexual activity.

- One in seventeen felt threatened or harassed (not related to sexual content).

- Girls were targeted at about twice the rate boys were targeted.

- Seventy-seven percent of targeted youth were over fourteen years old.

- Although 22 percent of targeted youth were ages ten to thirteen, this group was disproportionately distressed by the incident.

- Adults (most between the ages of eighteen and twenty-five) accounted for 24 percent of the sexual solicitations.

- Juveniles made 48 percent of the solicitations and 48 percent of the aggressive solicitations.

- Age was unknown for 27 percent of solicitors.

- Slightly more than two thirds of solicitations and online approaches came from males.

- One quarter of aggressive approaches were by females.

While not all the youth who received some sort of sexual solicitation online were bothered by the interaction, some (one in four of those solicited) were "very or extremely upset or afraid." The researchers found that few distressing online interactions are reported to parents, let alone police. To make matters more frustrating, even if parents report online harassment of their children, most police departments are ill equipped to follow up on such complaints and may view complaining parents as a nuisance. Issues of jurisdiction and arrest aside, most police departments lack the sophisticated computer skills required to retrieve digital evidence that will pass muster in court. Additionally, parents may balk at turning over their computer to police, either due to the inconvenience involved (including loss of the computer for a period of time) or possibly due to a fear that police may find something illegal on the hard drive and charge a member of the household with a crime. It is common knowledge that online child pornography arrests have stemmed from a computer being brought into a shop for repairs.

Victims and Predators

Using the same data collected in the New Hampshire study, researchers explored common characteristics of children they considered at risk for online sexual solicitation. Researchers found that girls, older teens, troubled youth, frequent Internet users, chat room participants, and children who communicate online with strangers were more likely than other children to be solicited online for sex.

A Florida man who owned and operated residential facilities for youths aged eleven to eighteen was arrested after he brought his computer in for repairs and child pornography was found on the hard drive. A well-known rock performer, Gary Glitter, was convicted in Britain of possessing child pornography after a repair shop discovered it on his hard drive. South Dakota (along with several other states) has passed a law requiring computer-repair shops to report any child pornography to authorities. Even without a law in place, many law-abiding individuals are fearful about having contact with anything resembling child pornography and will report such findings quickly to law enforcement. . . .

The online victim of the child molester is not really any different from the real-world victim, other than the fact that the victim is old enough to know how to use a computer and sufficiently literate to interact online. Such children generally tend to have low self-esteem, lack of (online) supervision, dysfunctional families, etc. While all of these traits may be common to the online victim, they are not required. An A-student with excellent self-esteem and a wonderful home life is not exempt from victimization by an online sexual predator. For example, a thirteen-year-old Minnesota eighth grader met a man she believed was eighteen through an AOL chat room before Christmas. They talked by phone prior to New Year's Eve, and she agreed to meet him near her home. She met a forty-year-old man who took her to a motel and gave her video games to play and wine coolers to drink. The man then allegedly raped the girl when she resisted his advances, A fifteen-year-old girl was found with a forty-three-year-old psychology professor in a New York State park, allegedly engaged in sexual intercourse in a car. The professor and the victim met online.

As noted earlier, the victim of an online sexual predator may have cooperated with the offender in one manner or another and may not cooperate with law enforcement. The victim may feel a sense of loyalty to the offender, may have participated in crimes (i.e., downloaded or traded child pornography), or may be simply generally rebellious and not fazed by the fact that [she]/he has been exploited. It may be difficult for investigators and prosecutors to relate to such a victim. Often, such a victim makes for a less than optimal witness. It is important for law enforcement personnel to refrain from being judgmental and accept the fact that gaining the cooperation of the victim may take a considerable amount of time. Judgmental treatment, disdain, and lack of interest by law enforcement toward such victims only reinforce their poor self-image and further victimize them for acts they engaged in but were poorly prepared for emotionally and were unable to give true informed consent. In an investigation of ten children identified through seized child pornography, for example, none of the ten reported the abuse they had endured to anyone without prompting.

The victims of the online sexual predator described above may differ somewhat from the victims of child pornography, whose pictures are distributed over the Internet. The victims described above are likely still living in the home, although that is no guarantee of safety. Child pornography victims are of various types: children and adolescents exploited by their guardians; victims offered alcohol and/or drugs and either videotaped without their knowledge committing sexual acts or performing under various kinds of ruses or threats; runaways seeking shelter or friendship with adolescents. The moral bankruptcy of those willing to exploit others knows no bounds. There are even clubs composed of parents who swap child pornography involving their own children with other like-minded individuals and child pornography distributors. It has been reported that live child-sex shows have even been sent over the Internet with viewers forwarding instructions to the adult participants as to what they would like to happen. . . .

How to Protect Children Online

It is not possible to ensure our children are safe from everyone at all times. But it is possible to take reasonable steps to protect our children while online. When we rely solely on educating children about Internet safety, we inadvertently place the responsibility for protecting our children on our children. Protecting children is the responsibility of their parents, the community, and government. Prevention efforts should incorporate components that educate parents, children, police officers, teachers, and health-care professionals.

Organizations such as the National Center for Missing and Exploited Children, PedoWatch, the Child Protection and Advocacy Coalition, getnetwise, and isafe offer information on how to protect children online and where to report trafficking in child pornography. Commercial software can monitor online behaviors, including e-mail, chat room conversations, instant messages, passwords, and Web site visits. Some software can even record keystrokes. Most monitoring software allows the installer to guard access to it with a password, and monitoring takes place unbeknownst to the user. The installer usually has the option of directing the monitoring software to send a report via e-mail that details all computer activity. Some monitoring software allows the installer to monitor the computer user's activity in real time from a remote location. Other software is engineered to allow the installer to conduct a forensic examination of the user's computer system from a remote location.

A frequently invoked misnomer in the online safety field is the concept of a "stranger." It is quite difficult to educate young children about the dangers of strangers when talking about the Internet. A stranger is someone a child does not know. Stranger-hood is easily overcome by child molesters. Even something as simple as using the child's name (perhaps overheard moments before) or asking for help in finding a lost puppy has been enough to overcome intensive "stranger danger" instruction by parents. Adolescents, on the other hand, have already had much experience dealing with adults they do not know. Prevention education efforts are well advised to encourage children and adolescents to feel comfortable in going to their parents or a trusted adult when in need of guidance. Teaching a child to "check with mom, dad, or a trusted adult" before going off with anyone is more helpful than saying, "don't ever talk to strangers." After all, if abducted, a child may be best served by turning to a stranger for help.

It is good to keep in mind that child abduction in general and Internet child molester abductions are actually rare phenomena. A child molester may be just as likely to meet an FBI agent at the planned rendezvous as a thirteen-year-old girl. While the problem of online predation is real, parents should not be in constant dread that their children will be attacked through the computer. They need to be aware of their children's online habits and who their friends are. It probably makes the most sense to educate children to the fact that some people in the world are willing to exploit them and, that when troubled by an interaction online (or in the real world), they should not be embarrassed to discuss the situation with a parent or other responsible adult.

CHAPTER 2

The Causes and Consequences of Child Abuse

Poverty Is a Factor in Child Neglect

Margaret G. Smith and Rowena Fong

In the following selection, a chapter from Children of Neglect: When No One Cares, *Margaret G. Smith and Rowena Fong assert that although poverty does not constitute child neglect, children who grow up in poverty are at much higher risk for neglect than those who do not. The U.S. Department of Health and Human Services (HHS) defines neglect as a failure to provide for a child's basic needs—deprivation of adequate food, clothing, shelter, supervision, education, or medical care. Child neglect is the most common form of child abuse; according to an HHS report, 60.9 percent of abused children in 2003 were victims of child neglect. Smith and Fong argue that poverty often results in children experiencing neglect through inadequate and unsafe housing, homelessness, domestic violence, and living in dangerous neighborhoods. The authors contend that it is society's responsibility to ensure that children are not deprived of their basic and emotional material needs.*

Margaret G. Smith is a social worker in private practice, with over thirty years' experience in child welfare and advocacy. Rowena Fong is professor of social work at the University of Texas at Austin. She teaches social work practice with children and families, child welfare, and family preservation.

Child neglect seriously injures and/or kills children at least as often as abuse.... Fifty-two percent of children who died as a result of maltreatment between 1993 and 1995 were victims of child neglect. Evidence also was presented that indicates that neglect is the most prevalent type of child mal-

treatment. It has been asserted that there is a strong association between child neglect and poverty, indicating that, while
poverty cannot be said to cause child neglect, it is the pre-
dominant risk factor. It is clear—children who grow up in
poverty are at higher risk for neglect than those who do not.
To the extent that poverty is the responsibility of the society
in which children live, society can be said to be neglectful in
not providing the resources that reduce risks for children. . . .

Statistics on Children Living in Poverty

In 1995 the federal government determined that a family of
three with an income below $12,156 per year was living in a
condition of poverty, in 1995 and 1996, 20%, one in five of all
children in the United States, lived in families that met this
criterion. The statistics are worse for children under the age of
six. One in every four preschoolers in the United States lives
in poverty. The rates are even higher for minority children,
children living in single-parent households, and children
whose parents did not finish high school. Approximately 15%
of White children live below the poverty line as compared to
54% of African-American children and 44% of Hispanic children. In addition, minority families experience more severe
and persistent poverty than do White families; they more frequently live in resource-poor neighborhoods; and their numbers are increasing proportionately, while the numbers for
White children are not. Irrespective of race, for children in
single-parent households, the poverty rate is 58%. It is almost
66% for children whose parents did not finish high school.

Extreme poverty (approximately $6,000 for a family of
three or $8,000 for a family of four) is the condition in which
8% of the children of the United States live. These figures indicate that over 14,000,000 children were classified as poor in
1995, and 5,600,000 children lived in conditions of extreme
poverty. The Federal Interagency Forum on Child and Family
Statistics (1998) found that 3.4% of children lived in house-

holds reporting that they did not have enough to eat. These households were more likely than not to be poor. Poor households were also more likely to include the 6% of children who are at risk of hunger, the 5% of children who experience moderate hunger, and the 1% of children who suffer severe hunger. The condition of poverty for children is not improving. [In *Child Abuse and Neglect: A Look at the States* (1997), M.R.] Petit and [P.A.] Curtis found that the percentage of children living in poverty rose from 14% in 1969 to 21% in 1995. In addition, [in *The Welfare of Children* (1994), D.] Lindsey reported that the poverty children endure has become increasingly severe. As a result, the risk of neglect for these children may also be increasing.

In comparison with other segments of U.S. society, children are the poorest. They are, as a whole, poorer than working-age adults and the elderly. . . . There is also a vast disparity between the poverty status of children in the United States and that of children in other industrialized nations. The United States has the dubious honor of ranking as the number one industrialized nation in the magnitude of the discrepancy between the rich and the poor; and as number one of sixteen industrialized nations for rates of children living in poverty conditions. . . .

Poverty and Children's Health

Income and poverty status are disturbingly related to children's health. The Federal Interagency Forum on Child and Family Statistics (1998) found significantly higher rates of activity limitation among poor children. They were also less likely to have received the standard battery of immunizations (e.g., DPT, MMR, polio, and flu) and thus were at higher risk for contracting these diseases. Poor children also have increased exposure to environmental hazards (e.g., lead and violence), which increases the risk of adverse health outcomes. When inner-city grandmothers gather to talk about their grandchildren's "numbers," they are not discussing SAT scores. They are discussing the children's blood lead levels.

Low-income families have significantly more moderate to severe hunger problems than more advantaged families. The effects of hunger and malnutrition can include fatigue, irritability, dizziness, frequent headaches, frequent colds and infections, and difficulty concentrating. As indicated earlier, two to four million children in the United States went hungry in the early 1990s. It is believed that these figures do not adequately represent the actual number of children experiencing food insufficiency and resultant malnutrition in the United States.

There is an important relationship between poverty and growth stunting. The stunting rate among poor children is approximately twice the expected rate. Children's dental health is also affected by their poverty status. [In a 1998 article in *The Future of Children*, E.M.] Lewit and N. Kerrebrock (1998) found that "poor children, because they are less likely than their wealthier peers to receive dental services, are at the highest risk of suffering the pain and consequences of untreated dental disease."

These outcomes are exacerbated by the aforementioned diminished access to health care that is associated with poverty; and are particularly problematic for the "near poor" who do not qualify for Medicaid and lack health insurance. In 1993, 20% of poor children lacked health insurance owing to the expansion of Medicaid and the retraction of private insurance. In an attempt to control costs, while expanding eligibility to meet the growing need, states have turned to Medicaid managed-care contracts, the effects of which on the quality of health care for the poor are not yet known.

Poverty, Mental Health, and Child Development

Children who live in poor rural areas, and are serviced by the child welfare and/or juvenile justice systems, are the children who are most at risk for mental health problems. Moreover, rural families' economic problems are most destructive for children's mental health and functioning when those problems are chronic and seemingly without solutions. [In a 2001 article in the journal *Development and Psychopathology,* K.E.] Bolger and [C.J.] Patterson found increased internalizing of problems and perceived external locus of control in children living in conditions of economic hardship. Thus these children were at risk for depression and anxiety disorders, and felt they had little impact on their environment.

Poverty and the related increase in life-stressing events, including faulty parenting, can have major adverse effects on children's cognitive and social development. Poverty-related factors such as lead poisoning and malnutrition can contribute to poor outcomes for children's cognitive development as well as their health and physical development. In addition, population-based risk factors related to poverty other than inadequate nutrition can also contribute to poor performance on tests of cognitive ability.

There is a strong association between poverty occurring early in a child's life and high school graduation. Low income during the preschool and early school years exhibits the strongest correlation with low rates of high school completion. In addition to not completing school, children's school performance suffers when they are living in conditions of poverty. On February 18, 2000, the *New York Times* reported that children living in poverty were less likely to be able to count to ten, recite the alphabet, or be in good health than their more advantaged cohorts. In addition to being an effect of poverty itself, poor health plays a part in children's school performance. Healthy youngsters are more likely to come to school and pay attention.

Poverty, Stress, and Parenting

Evidence has related poverty to child abuse and neglect. It is through the material hardship that poverty causes that poverty is likely to have an impact on children and families. Pre-occupied with the stresses and difficulties of living in conditions of material deprivation, parents, usually single women, have trouble responding to their children's needs. These same stressors and difficulties render parents, themselves, vulnerable to psychological distress, depression, and anxiety. These factors can lead to adverse parenting, which, in turn, has negative outcomes for children. The harmful effects of poverty may therefore, in part, be transmitted to children by its harmful effects on their caretakers, usually their mothers.

Single, teenage mothers are overrepresented among the poor and are at greater risk for negative parenting behaviors. They tend to be more insensitive and impatient with their infants, have less realistic expectations, and provide less responsive, less stimulating, and less affectionate environments for their children. Their children more consistently display vulnerability to negative outcomes, indicating that the age and marital status of parents can exacerbate the already high risks faced by children who live in poverty.

The solutions to the problems of poverty, in themselves, can result in adverse parenting and negative outcomes for children. Welfare-to-work programs may force parents out of their homes; and, in the absence of child care, children are left home alone. Food budgets may have to be cut, resulting in hungry children. Child neglect, associated with these behaviors (i.e., lack of supervision, malnutrition), may result in foster care placement for children. The positive effects of mothers working out of the home can be undermined by low wages, repetitive jobs, poor working conditions, and inadequate child care. Research has indicated that, given these circumstances, children's home experiences begin to deteriorate, becoming less stimulating and nurturing.

Poverty also influences the levels of paternal involvement with children. Fathers in poor families are less emotionally and behaviorally involved in their children's lives; and the greater the persistence of poverty, the less fathers are involved.

Even when fathers are involved, there are few buffering effects of fathers in poor families. These findings regarding adverse parenting indicate that poor children are more at risk for child abuse and neglect; unsupportive, unstimulating, and chaotic home environments; poor family management practices; and severe family disruption, including placement out of the home.

Future Outcomes

As indicated earlier, children raised in poverty are less likely to graduate from high school. In view of the fact that the poverty rate for families in which the parent(s) did not graduate from high school is 66%, lack of a high school degree places these children at risk of remaining in poverty as adults. Children raised in poverty are more likely to be unemployed at age nineteen than nonpoor children. African-American boys raised in the inner cities have less of a chance to reach adulthood than their more advantaged peers. As can be seen, being raised in poverty can severely limit children's life prospects.

In conclusion, our children are our future. We have provided for the health and income security of our elderly; now it is time to do the same for our children. We certainly have the capacity to do so. The question is: do we have the will? If we do not, it is our future that is at stake. If we do not reduce the risks to children living in poverty, we will not have the skilled workers needed to drive our market economy in the future. Instead there will be an ever-increasing welfare class. No society can survive that is not interested in ensuring the well-being of the next generation. We must care for our children now, if for no other reason than to secure our own future.

Substance-Abusing Parents Are More Likely to Abuse Their Children

Joseph A. Califano Jr.

An epidemic of parental drug and alcohol abuse has caused a catastrophic increase in child abuse that has pushed the child welfare system to the brink of collapse, writes Joseph A. Califano Jr., the president of the National Center on Addiction and Substance Abuse at Columbia University in New York City. According to Califano, parents who are substance abusers are three times more likely to physically or sexually assault their children, and children of such parents are four times more likely to be victims of neglect. If there is to be any hope of preventing child abuse and preserving the natural family unit, he maintains, child welfare workers must be trained to detect substance abuse. Moreover, Califano argues, parents who abuse drugs and alcohol must be offered a comprehensive rehabilitation program that centers on substance abuse treatment, parenting skills, job training, and physical and mental health care.

Consider the following for a measure of national self-indulgence in the midst of the longest and greatest economic boom in our history. We Americans spend more on cosmetic surgery, hairpieces and make-up *for men* than we do on child welfare services for battered and neglected children of substance-abusing parents.

A tornado of drug and alcohol abuse and addiction is tearing through the nation's child welfare and family court systems, leaving in its path the wreckage of abused and neglected children, turning social welfare agencies and courts on their heads and uprooting the traditional disposition to keep children with their natural parents.

There is no safe haven for these abused and neglected children of drug- and alcohol-abusing parents. They are the most vulnerable and endangered individuals in America. That is the grim conclusion of an exhaustive two-year analysis by The National Center on Addiction and Substance Abuse at Columbia University [CASA.]

Drugs and Alcohol Are Fueling an Epidemic of Child Abuse

Parental alcohol and drug abuse and addiction have pushed the nation's system of child welfare to the brink of collapse. From 1986 to 1997, the number of abused and neglected children in America has soared from 1.4 million to some 3 million, a stunning 114.3 percent jump, more than eight times faster than the 13.9 percent increase in the overall children's population. The number of *reported* abused and neglected children who have been killed has climbed from 798 in 1985 to 1,185 in 1996; the U.S. Advisory Board on Child Abuse and Neglect sets the *actual* number much higher, at 2,000, a rate of more than five deaths a day.

Alcohol, crack cocaine, methamphetamine, heroin and marijuana are fueling this population explosion of battered and neglected children. Children whose parents abuse drugs and alcohol are almost three times likelier to be physically or sexually assaulted and more than four times likelier to be neglected than children of parents who are not substance abusers. The parent who abuses drugs and alcohol is often a child who was abused by alcohol- and drug-abusing parents.

Eighty percent of professionals surveyed by CASA said that substance abuse causes or exacerbates most of the cases of child abuse and neglect they face. Nine of 10 professionals cite alcohol alone or in combination with illegal or prescrip-

Parents who abuse drugs or alcohol are more likely to become violent and abuse their families. © Tom and Dee Ann McCarthy/CORBIS

tion drugs as the leading substance of abuse in child abuse and neglect; 45.8 percent cite crack cocaine as the leading illegal substance of abuse; 20.5 percent cite marijuana (which can hardly be considered a benign drug in this situation).

Parental substance abuse and addiction is the chief culprit in at least 70 percent—and perhaps 90 percent—of all child welfare spending—some $10 billion of the $14 billion that Federal, state and local governments spent simply to maintain child welfare systems in 1998. This $10 billion does not include the costs of health care to abused and neglected children, operating law enforcement and judicial systems consumed with this problem, treating developmental problems, providing special education or lost productivity. Nor does it include the costs attributable to child abuse and neglect that are privately incurred. These costs easily add another $10 billion to the price of child abuse and neglect.

The human costs are incalculable: broken families; children who are malnourished; babies who are neglected, beaten and sometimes killed by alcohol- and crack-addicted parents; eight-year-olds sent out to steal or buy drugs for addicted parents: sick children wallowing in unsanitary conditions; child victims of sodomy, rape and incest; children in such agony and despair that they themselves resort to drugs or alcohol for relief.

Alcohol and drugs have blown away the topsoil of family life and reshaped the landscape of child abuse and neglect in America. Parents addicted to drugs and alcohol are clever at hiding their addiction and are often more concerned about losing their access to drugs and being punished than about losing custody of their children.

Motivation

For some parents, holding onto their children can provide the motivation to seek treatment. But for many the most insidious aspect of substance abuse and addiction is their power to destroy the natural parental instinct to love and care for their children. Eighty-six percent of professionals surveyed cited lack of motivation as the top barrier to getting such parents into treatment. As Alan Leshner, director of the National Institute on Drug Abuse, has observed, the addicted parent sometimes sees the child as an obstacle to getting drugs.

Parental drug and alcohol abuse and addiction have overwhelmed the child welfare system. By 1997 some caseworkers were responsible for 50 cases of child maltreatment at any one time and judges were handling as many as 50 cases a day, giving them less than 10 minutes in an uninterrupted eight-hour day to assess the testimony of parents, social workers, law enforcement officers and others in determining a child's fate.

Child welfare agencies have been forced to allocate more time to investigations, gathering evidence of neglect and abuse of children by alcohol- and drug-involved parents. This shift in focus has changed the way parents and children see caseworkers and the way these caseworkers view themselves. This shift also threatens to criminalize a process that should be driven by treatment, health care and compassion for both parent and child. The frantic response of many in Congress . . . is to add felonies to the Federal criminal code and throw more parents in prison—actions likely to do more harm than good for the children of these parents, who need stable and secure homes.

Few caseworkers and judges who make decisions about these children have been tutored in substance abuse and addiction. There are no national estimates of the gap between those parents who need treatment and those who receive it, but Federal Government surveys show that two-thirds of all individuals who need treatment do not get it. There is nothing to suggest that these substance-abusing parents fare any better than the general population.

As the role of substance abuse has increased, the age of the victimized children has gone down. Today most cases of abuse and neglect by substance-abusing parents involve children under five. Alcohol use and binge drinking during pregnancy are up, with at least 636,000 expectant mothers drinking and 137,000 drinking heavily. Some 500,000 babies born each year have been exposed in their mother's womb to cocaine and other illicit drugs (and usually alcohol and tobacco as well). Each year some 20,000 infants are abandoned at birth or kept at hospitals to protect them from substance-abusing parents. The proportion of children whom caseworkers place in foster care at birth jumped 44 percent from the 1983–86 period to the 1990–94 period.

Drug and alcohol abuse has thrown into doubt a fundamental tenet of child welfare workers: the commitment to keep the child with his or her natural parents. While terminating parental rights has long been viewed as a failure, alcohol, crack cocaine and other forms of drug abuse have challenged this time-honored precept.

Lost Opportunities

There is an irreconcilable clash between the rapidly ticking clock of physical, intellectual, emotional and spiritual development for the abused and neglected child and the slow-motion clock of recovery for the parent addicted to alcohol or drugs. For the cognitive development of young children, weeks are windows of opportunity that can never be reopened. For the parent, recovery from drug or alcohol addiction takes time—and relapse, especially during initial periods of recovery, is common.

Bluntly put, the time that parents need to conquer their substance abuse and addiction can pose a serious threat to their children who may suffer permanent damage during this phase of rapid development. Little children cannot wait; they need safe and stable homes and nurturing adults *now* in order to set the stage for a healthy and productive life.

The cruelest dimension of this tragedy for children abused by parents using drugs and alcohol is this: Even when parental rights are terminated in a timely way for such parents who refuse to enter treatment or who fail to recover, in our self-indulgent society there is no assurance of a safe haven for the children. There are not nearly enough adoptive homes. Being in foster care, while far better than being abused, rarely offers the lasting and secure nurturing for full cognitive development—and appropriate foster care is also in short supply. More caring, responsible adults need to step forward to care for the least among us, children of substance-abusing parents.

Child welfare systems and practices need a complete overhaul. Social service providers, from agency directors to front-line child welfare workers, judges, court clerks, masters, lawyers, and health and social service staffs need intensive training in the nature and detection of substance abuse and what to do when they spot it. In all investigations of child abuse and neglect, parents should be screened and assessed for substance abuse. Caseworkers and judges should move rapidly to place children for adoption when parents refuse treatment or fail to respond to it. We need to increase greatly the incentives for foster care and adoption and the number of judges and caseworkers.

Comprehensive Treatment Is a Must

Comprehensive treatment that is timely and appropriate, especially for substance-abusing mothers, is essential to prevent further child abuse and neglect. Treatment must be part of a concentrated course that would include mental health services and physical health care; literacy, job and parenting skills training; as well as socialization, employment and drug-free housing. Since most fathers have walked out on their responsibilities, such treatment must be attentive to the fact that most of these parents are women. Where the only hope of re-constituting the natural family for the abused child rests in comprehensive treatment for the parent, it is an inexcusable and vicious Catch-22 situation not to make such treatment available.

Of course, this all costs money. Can we afford to do these things? In the most affluent nation in the history of the world, the answer is a loud and clear yes. Failure to protect these children and provide treatment for their parents who fall prey to drugs and alcohol is more likely than any other shortcoming of survival-of-the-fittest capitalism to bring the harsh judgment of God and history upon us.

In recent years, Pope John Paul II [had] repeatedly reminded capitalist nations to soften the sharp edges that cut up the least among them. What better way to heed that admonition than to give the needs of these parents and their children first call on the burgeoning Federal budget surplus and the money that the states are picking up from the tobaco settlement.

How Abusive Parents Justify Child Maltreatment

Gregory K. Moffatt

In the following viewpoint, Gregory K. Moffatt explains how some parents are able to commit cruelties against their children. Arguing that ignorance, poor coping skills, substance abuse, and sheer viciousness are factors in child abuse, Moffatt suggests that parents use psychological defense mechanisms—such as denial, rationalization, and justification—to excuse their abusive behavior to themselves and others.

The author of Wounded Innocents and Fallen Angels: Child Abuse and Child Aggression, A Violent Heart: Understanding Aggressive Individuals, *and* Blind-Sided: Homicide Where It Is Least Expected, *Gregory K. Moffatt is a professor of psychology at Atlanta Christian College. He is also a therapist in private practice, specializing in children, violence, and aggression.*

It seems inconceivable that a parent or guardian could deliberately harm a child or neglect a child's needs, yet perusal of the national news reveals the unmistakable truth that such thoughtlessness and cruelty exist. Psychologically, we can look to a number of reasons why parents abuse their children. Three of these reasons are termed *defense mechanisms* because they are ways in which people psychologically defend themselves from their self-perceived weaknesses. Denial, rationalization, and justification are these three. Other psychological reasons that contribute to abuse are ignorance, poor problem-solving skills, poor coping skills, substance abuse, and cruelty.

Denial is a defense mechanism where one refuses to believe the obvious. Abusing parents may deny that they are abusing a child by pretending that their behavior is not abusive or by denying that they are doing anything to the child at all. When officials intervene on a child's behalf, the denying abuser is obvious because no matter what evidence of abuse social workers provide—broken bones, scars, burns, and so forth—the abuser excuses that evidence, dismisses it, or discounts its seriousness. . . .

[The concept of] abuse [is] partially culture-bound. Prior to the mid-1960s, it was not uncommon for parents to use corporal punishment. In even earlier decades, severe use of corporal punishment was not uncommon, even if it left marks such as bruises. Parents were not being cruel or abusive by the standards of the day. They were simply using the method of discipline that the culture at that time accepted as appropriate. Now, in a new millennium, any punishment that leaves marks of any kind is cause for suspicion of abuse. The culture has changed and methods of punishment that were once acceptable are no longer acceptable. Therefore, an accused abuser from an earlier generation may truly not understand his or her abuse in this new age. Officials involved in intervention should be sensitive to this possibility when charging an individual with a crime or when providing intervention or treatment.

Rationalization

A second defense mechanism that contributes to abuse is rationalization. With this defense, one uses false logic to explain away seemingly inappropriate behavior, making it appear acceptable. Most of us use this defense at one time or another. We might argue on the one hand that it is wrong to exceed the speed limit when we drive, yet when we get behind the wheel, we exceed the speed limit. We "reason" that we aren't really speeding as long as we are within a certain number of miles per hour over the speed limit. Or we may argue that everyone else is speeding; therefore, our behavior is acceptable.

On a fast-moving interstate, we might argue that it is danger-ous to drive the speed limit because everyone else is driving so fast that they might run over us. All these excuses are ratio-nalizations and are based on false logic. In other words, we have to juxtapose two opposing truths—our belief that speed-ing is wrong and yet we speed.

Abusers rationalize in the same way—excusing their be-havior by using false logic. They might say they don't "ordi-narily" lose their temper and strike a child, as if it is accept-able to do that once in a while. Or they might argue that they were "disciplined" like that when they were children and they "turned out all right." With these rationalized explanations, the abuser is ignoring the primary issue—what is best for the child.

Justification

Justification, a third defense mechanism, is a defense where one excuses behaviors based on some perceived "permission." In World War II, for example, guards in the Nazi death camps justified their inhumane treatment of inmates by arguing that they were simply "following orders." The fact that they were following orders gave them permission to be cruel. Likewise, . . . members of hate groups justify their hatred by contending that they have been called by God to maim or destroy other humans. The most egregious example of justification in recent history came in September 2001—the terrorist attacks on the Pentagon and the World Trade Center's twin towers. The per-petrators believed they were justified in killing thousands of people and causing billions of dollars in damage because they perceived themselves to be engaged in a holy war—a jihad—commissioned by God to rid the earth of infidels.

Abusers justify their behavior by these same means. They may argue that they are only disciplining the child, hence giv-ing themselves permission to harm a child. Or they may be-lieve that a child "asked for" the abuse because of deliberate misbehavior. Abusers, like terrorists, may even believe that God has called them to beat or neglect a child. In 2000 in Atlanta, Georgia, an entire church congregation came under the scrutiny of the Department of Family and Children's Services (DFACS) because of abuse that had been alleged. These members were publicly flogging one another's children. Even after social services removed more than forty of these children, the families refused to agree to stop the behaviors that the state had determined to be abusive, arguing that they could not deny what they believed to be a religious command. Obviously, there is flawed logic operating in all of these examples, but the abuser either does not see it or chooses to ignore it.

Ignorance

Some caregivers abuse or neglect their children simply because they aren't very bright, they are immature, or they do not know any better. Especially among the poor and uneducated, parents may neglect or abuse their children because they have never been taught effective ways to discipline and care for their children. Very young parents are more likely to be abusive than older parents because younger parents may only have found yelling, hitting, or ignoring as effective ways of disciplining their children. Older parents, on the other hand, have learned a number of ways to gain compliance from their children. I have worked with many parents over the years who have abused or neglected their children and when they realized what they were doing, they were more than willing to try something new. Education and training often resolved the problems.

Poor Problem-Solving Skills

Problem-solving skills are those cognitive activities that we use to achieve our goals. When we run out of ideas for solving a problem, we experience frustration, and frustration leads to anger. Caregivers who have minimal problem-solving skills quickly become frustrated with children when they do not cooperate. Many infants have been injured or killed by something called "shaken baby syndrome." A baby's head is heavy in proportion to its body and infants do not have strength enough in the neck to support that weight. Shaking the infant causes the head to jerk back and forth, and can easily injure the base of the brain. Frustrated caregivers run out of ways to deal with a crying child and, in their frustration, they shake the child. This is obviously an ineffective strategy for solving the problem of a crying infant, but in the midst of crisis, the abusing parent does not recognize that fact or does not know what else to do.

Several years ago I was forced to call the county Department of Family and Children's Services (DFACS) because a family I was working with was clearly neglecting their four children. The youngest child was just over one year of age and the eldest was eight. The father worked long hours and, therefore, was gone much of the time. The mother was very young and she was easily stressed. Daily, she would lock herself in her bedroom, leaving the children unattended for hours at a time. One day, I was driving near their home and saw a child sitting literally in the middle of the roadway, cars passing on either side. Just by chance it was the youngest child of this family that I knew. I stopped my vehicle, removed the child from the roadway, and took her home. The mother was locked in her bedroom asleep, completely unaware that the child had even left the house, not to mention sitting in the middle of a busy roadway. Clearly, the mother's problem-solving strategy of hiding in her room was both ineffective and inappropriate. Part of her treatment involved learning more effective ways to cope with her stress, depression, loneliness, and frustrations with her children. . . .

Poor Coping Skills

I cannot see how anyone in mental health could address any dysfunction without considering [coping skills.] Coping skills are the strategies and tools that we use to help us deal with the stress we face in life. In early years, children have very few coping skills. They scream, whine, or cry if they are uncomfortable or if their immediate needs are not being met. As children age, they learn some coping skills through direct instructions. That is, they are given specific directions by parents, teachers, or other adults as to how they can learn to cope with their difficulties. For example, a parent who intervenes in a fight between children and says, "Next time you are angry you should first . . ." is teaching the child a coping skill. Other coping skills are acquired through trial and error. Often, adults may find themselves in their thirties or forties before they develop coping strategies that are fully functional in helping them deal with their rage, depression, or frustrations.

When coping skills are absent or ineffective, the individual becomes frustrated. When the parent runs out of coping skills, he or she is most likely to strike a child. Some parents think they have effective coping skills, but they do not. They make the mistake of assuming that just because they use a given coping strategy regularly, that it is an effective one. For example, one parent I worked with who had anger-management problems told me, "I always spank when I'm angry." To him, that seemed like a perfectly reasonable justification for his physical aggression toward his children, even though it was both ineffective and inappropriate.

Baby temperament may also contribute to abuse in infants. Research has demonstrated that there are three major temperaments in infants—easy, slow-to-warm, and difficult. Most babies are easy or slow-to-warm and like to be snuggled, and even though they will cry with some frequency, they are quickly calmed if their needs are met. Researchers, however, identified a small percentage of babies as "difficult" babies. These children do not like to be held, snuggled, or coddled. They cry most of their waking hours and, regardless of a parent's good intentions, they are not easily calmed. Anyone who has ever walked a fussy baby at two o'clock in the morning can relate to how frustrating it is when the baby cannot be mollified. Parents who have poor problem-solving skills and/or poor coping skills will become frustrated more quickly and are more likely to strike or shake a child, thereby causing injury.

Single parents are also at a disadvantage. In a two-parent home, part of the coping strategy is to pass responsibility to the other parent when one's stress level rises. This is not an option for single parents. This, combined with the fact that many very young parents are unmarried, increases the likelihood of abuse by young parents.

Substance Abuse

The probability for child abuse increases significantly if substance abuse is present in the home. Nearly half of all substantiated cases of abuse involve some form of parental substance abuse. The risk of child maltreatment is even greater in single-parent homes. Chemical addictions reduce one's ability to function, think rationally, and engage in the normal business of life. Addicted individuals will neglect all responsibilities in the pursuit of their drug. Alcohol reduces inhibitions and increases the likelihood of uncontrolled rage. When that rage is directed at a defenseless child, the results are devastating. While no abuse is acceptable, children of alcoholics or other substance abusers are more likely to suffer injuries than children who are maltreated in homes where alcohol is not an issue.

Cruelty

Some people are cruel. They are heartless, selfish, and egocentric, pursuing their own pleasures even at the expense of their own children. These sadistic people delight in controlling and manipulating other people and they have no remorse for their behavior when they are caught. Cruel people will abuse children "just because they feel like it" or even for entertainment. For example, a man in Missouri was arrested for burning a kitten on his outdoor grill just for the fun of it while nearly a dozen friends watched and laughed at the helpless kitten. To me, people like this are as frightening as any serial killer and anyone who finds pleasure in this kind of cruelty is seriously disturbed. Fortunately, most abusers do not fall exclusively into this category.

Considering Cultural Context When Determining Child Abuse

Lisa Aronson Fontes

In the following article, Lisa Aronson Fontes, a psychologist who has worked for more than fifteen years to make social service agencies and mental health systems more responsive to culturally diverse families, discusses the cultural factors to consider when determining whether a child is being abused. Noting that, for example, parents would not be accused of neglect if their child refused to eat her cereal and was hungry at school or broke his arm playing football, Fontes argues that different cultures have traditions that might complicate a finding of abuse. Fontes discusses common "false positives"—findings of abuse when none is present—as well as "false negatives," in which the perpetrator of abuse attempts to use culture to mask child maltreatment. When working with culturally diverse families, Fontes cautions, it is best to ask questions and not make assumptions about whether a behavior is "normal" in a particular cultural context.

Determining whether a given act constitutes child maltreatment may seem like a straightforward process, but often it is not. How much harm is too much? . . . Exposure to many hours of television has been found to harm children's cognitive achievement and contribute to obesity, and yet few would argue that caretakers who allow their children to watch many hours of television are abusive. And how much risk is too much? . . . If a kindergartener breaks his arm while playing unsupervised in a stairwell, his parents may be subject to sanctions for neglect. However, if the same parents allow their child to ski and he breaks his arm, this is not considered neglectful. Clearly, cultural norms shape how we evaluate abuse and risk. . . .

False positives in child welfare often result from ethnocentrism, where the professional sees his or her own beliefs and practices as superior, and misidentifies differing cultural practices as maltreatment. When ethnocentrism prevails, the beliefs and behaviors of the dominant culture are imposed on other populations, and nonmainstream childcare practices are mistakenly viewed as pathological, even when there is no harm to children.

"False Positives" and Sleeping Arrangements

Some families from traditional peasant cultures in Asia, Africa, and South America are incorrectly substantiated for neglect because their children sleep on the floor. Before substantiating such a claim it would be important to determine whether this practice is traditional in the family's country of origin, whether the parents also sleep on the floor, and whether the sleeping space on the floor is clean and sanitary. Some Asian families use clean and comfortable mats for sleeping on the floor that they roll up each morning, leaving investigators scratching their heads as they search for beds.

Families may be incorrectly found to be negligent or suspected of sexual abuse because they share beds, when sharing a bed may be customary in their country of origin and should not be seen in and of itself as being indicative of sexual abuse. In some countries, such as Korea, it is traditional for the mother to sleep with her children in a room separate from the father who sleeps alone. (However, of course, even if sharing a bed or a hammock may be customary, sexual abuse *still* could be occurring.) Additionally, while it is common for children in families who share close quarters to be exposed to the sounds of their parents' lovemaking, this exposure might still be experienced by the child as uncomfortable and even abusive.

Co-sleeping itself may be problematic when children are beginning to mature physically and become aware of sexual urges, or if the adults have poor boundaries. Under normal circumstances, co-sleeping of nursing mothers with their infants facilitates nursing and the mother-child bond and should not be seen as problematic. Indeed, such co-sleeping may enhance the mother's ability to nurse and meet her child's needs. . . .

In most of the world's cultures children sleep in the same bed or at least the same room as their parents. People from cultures as diverse as the Maya of Mexico, the Iu Mien of Southeast Asia, and different groups in East Africa respond in horror when they hear that children in the United States and Canada are often expected to sleep in a room alone, either from birth or from a very young age. . . .

"False Positives" and Flexible Family Boundaries

Unlike middle-class and upper-middle-class persons from the dominant cultural groups, people with a low income and people from many immigrant groups often have fluid boundaries around their selves and around their household. In describing Latino families, [C.J.] Falicov has referred to this as the *familial self*, "a sense of self that includes one's close relationships as part of who one is" [*Latino Families in Therapy* (1998)]. [In an essay in E.P. Salett and D.R. Koslow's *Race, Ethnicity and Self* (1994), A.] Roland has also used the term "familial self" to describe Japanese and Indian people. When people have this extended sense of self, they may be more apt to share their homes, money, clothing, and even beds with relatives and family friends. . . . Among traditional families, this sharing of resources is not subject to debate; it is just what one does.

Sharing resources in this way creates a wider safety net than that provided by the societal institutions at large, thereby enabling families that may be stressed or near the poverty line to survive. Families may share meals, child- or elder care, transportation, and other resources. However, the fluidity of household boundaries can create dilemmas for the investigator who has learned to view the presence of adults other than parents as a risk factor. . . .

The issue of fluid household composition might emerge in a different way. A family may hesitate to tell investigators the full truth about who lives in their home. They might describe their nuclear family only, knowing that this is the norm in their new country. Only after trust has been built will they reveal that an additional family shares the apartment, or that friends or even renters are sleeping in the kids' room and that the kids are all sharing a bed in another room. . . .

Small Size or Failure to Thrive?

Sometimes young immigrant children are labeled as "failure to thrive" because of their low weight and small size. Children from ethnic groups whose people typically have a smaller stature than people from the dominant culture (including people from the Indian subcontinent, Asians, and Central Americans) may not approach U.S. norms and yet may be perfectly healthy. It would be important to investigate the child's overall health, and not rely on weight and size as sole indicators of growth problems. Additionally, children who breast-feed exclusively typically gain weight in a different pattern than their bottle-fed counterparts (although there are clear advantages to breast-feeding for the babies' health). A breast-feeding child of immigrants may appear "behind" his or her U.S. peers in terms of growth, but this may not be an indication of ill health or neglect.

Culture, Appearance, and Hygiene

Appearance influences how others see us and how we see them. . . . From clothing, we may make assumptions about a person's gender, age, occupation, level of hygiene, marital status, sexual orientation, and socioeconomic status. These assumptions can prove problematic if they form part of a child maltreatment assessment and are made without awareness of cultural variations.

Orthodox Jews first cut their children's hair at a party on the child's third birthday. Until this age, a child's hair is allowed to grow freely, so it may look unkempt to the uninformed outsider. Some Muslims, Native Americans, Rastafarians from Jamaica, and members of other ethnic and religious groups have restrictions around the cutting of hair that may make investigators believe the children are poorly groomed when in fact they are groomed in the way their culture dictates.

Additionally, many cultures have restrictions on bathing. During the week after the death of a loved one, Orthodox Jews typically tear their clothing and may not bathe, attend synagogue, work, sit in normal chairs, or look in mirrors. This is intended to help them face their grief, rather than burying it along with the loved one. Those closest to the person who died are forbidden to cut their hair or shave their beards for a month after the death. Other cultures have similar restrictions related to death, illness, or childbearing. In some cultures, women and girls are told to avoid bathing during menstruation, for fear that it could make them ill.

People from diverse cultures and religions may wear amulets or religious or superstitious objects that puzzle the investigator. A Portuguese man, for instance, may carry a peeled clove of garlic in his pocket at all times to keep away the *mal olhado* (evil eye). Hindu children may wear a thread around their torsos or wrists that should not be removed except in an annual ceremony. Native American children may have markings on their bodies or objects tied onto them, to protect them or to ensure healing after they've been ill. Gypsy (Roma) children and adults usually wear an amulet around their necks. In infancy, many Latin American and other Roman Catholic children are given necklaces or bracelets with crosses or medallions of saints, which they are instructed never to remove. Investigators should not interpret as problematic what may seem like an unusually strong commitment to the children keeping these objects on their bodies. After all, parents give children these objects to protect them—to show they care. . . .

Lack of Cooperation with Authorities

Families are sometimes "punished" by having their children removed because they are seen as unmotivated or uncooperative. Conversely, some children are not afforded adequate protection because abusive parents know how to play the system. Clearly, the more one knows about the workings of the system, the easier it is to follow the (often unwritten) rules, which puts immigrant families and other families who are not from the dominant group at a disadvantage.

There are, of course, many reasons why a family might fail to "cooperate" or comply with a treatment plan, and therefore run the risk of losing custody of their children. For people who do not speak English very well, they may not understand the treatment plan. Even if they understand the words, they may not understand some of the concepts (e.g., "seek developmentally appropriate opportunities"). [In "Families with Asian Roots," an essay in E.W. Lynch and M.J. Hanson's *Developing Cross-Cultural Competence* (1992), S.] Chan describes a Vietnamese mother who attended only intermittently an early intervention program that was deemed essential for the development of her 2 ½-year-old autistic child. With sensitive inquiry, the professional was able to determine that the mother had not understood what autism was or the importance of the intervention program. (No written information had been provided for her in Vietnamese and the interpreter did not know how to say the word "autism" in Vietnamese.) Additionally, the mother did not feel comfortable intensively stimulating her daughter verbally and socially in the way that was expected in the program—in her culture such stimulation was considered "unnatural and inappropriate" relative to the child's age and level of understanding. And finally, the mother was uneasy in the class because of her poor English-speaking skills. Fortunately, she was later given the opportunity to participate in a similar program with other Vietnamese parents, where both she and her child flourished. . . .

Unfamiliar Practices

Familiarity with a culture helps us distinguish between punishment techniques that are typical and those that are unusual. If you are not familiar with a given culture's disciplinary norms, I encourage you to seek consultation with professionals who come from the culture in question. Recently, a social worker told me that she had substantiated a charge of child abuse against Mexican American parents who had forced their children to kneel on uncooked rice as a punishment. (This is a common disciplinary practice among some Asian and Latino groups; in Spanish, it is called *hincar*.) Although the mark from the rice on the bare knees vanished quickly and the parents made their children kneel for no longer than 10 minutes at a time, the social worker said the practice seemed so bizarre that she thought it might have been a sign of the parents' mental illness and so she substantiated. A quick call to anyone familiar with Latino cultures or a consultation with a relevant text would have revealed that this disciplinary practice is ubiquitous in many Latin American countries, and should not be considered abusive unless it is used for long periods of time or in unusual ways.

Many traditional medical practices can be mistaken for abuse, including coining, cupping, and moxibustion. State protective agencies vary in how they handle these cases. [In *Traditional Medicine and Child Abuse* (2003), I.] Duong reports that in California traditional medicine that leaves a mark, such as coining, is not considered a form of child abuse. However, she reports that when a child is found to have bruising caused by a caretaker, even if this is thought to stem from a traditional medical practice, an investigation must be undertaken every time. She explains this policy to parents; she says that by the second or third visit by protective social workers, most Vietnamese, Laotian, and Cambodian parents will forego coining their children to avoid the hassle and suspicion engendered by the visit.

Families from minority cultures may not understand mainstream U.S. medical explanations and practices. Or—in their efforts to provide the care they trust most for their children— they may forego recommended Western procedures and rely instead on techniques and healers from their own culture. It is not uncommon for Asian families to readjust the dosages of prescription medicine or to stop taking medicine when the symptoms of an illness have disappeared, for instance. This fits their traditional view of how illnesses work—as being due to an imbalance of yin and yang. Antibiotics are seen as yang, and so Chinese patients frequently stop taking them when the symptoms vanish. Thus many Chinese parents believe that giving their child antibiotics for too long could make the child overly yang and provoke further problems. If the child's welfare depends on complying with a medical practice, then professionals may well have to enforce its use. But the questioning or rejection of medical care due to cultural beliefs should not be mistaken for simple neglect.

Parents may engage in practices with their children that investigators have trouble understanding, and therefore substantiate as abuse. For example:

I have a friend, Sajjan, who is a practicing Sikh. (Sikhism is a religion from India that believes in one God and the equality of all people.) Sajjan and her family . . . swaddle their children up to age 2 during naptime. "Swaddling" means wrapping a child snuggly in a long blanket or cloth so the child cannot move his or her limbs. . . . A neighbor saw one of her swaddled toddlers and called protective services. A claim of child abuse was substantiated against her. The investigator later admitted that she was completely unfamiliar with the practice of swaddling and found the house "odd," with its shoes lined up at the door, its people all dressed in white, and the faint scent of incense in the air. . . .

False Negatives: "My Culture Made Me Do It"

Sometimes, professionals can *fail* to recognize a given practice as maltreatment because of cultural differences between the investigator and the family. . . . Indeed, cultures successfully meet children's basic needs such as food, shelter, education, and socialization into adulthood in myriad ways. However, this does *not* mean that anything goes, as long as it is "cultural." Some cultural practices are harmful.

For example, in the United States children watch an average of 25 hours of television each week—television that is full of commercials and portrayals of violent acts. It could be argued that watching enormous quantities of television is a cultural norm in the United States, and yet few would say this is desirable for children. The same could be said for the U.S. cultural practice of feeding large quantities of fatty foods to children, so that more than 20% of children are obese. Other cultures and nations also engage in cultural practices that are harmful to children. . . . The list includes but is not limited to genital cutting; cures involving contact with mercury, lead, or other toxic substances; punishments that involve ingesting pepper or washing children's mouths out with soap or other irritating substances; corporal punishment; applying animal feces or lead-based kohl to an unhealed umbilical cord; discrimination against girls that results in underfeeding of girl children; child labor, child marriage, child sexual slavery, and prostitution; and so on. Some of these practices are obviously harmful, while others are less obviously harmful. Understanding what is cultural is no easy task. In efforts to be culturally sensitive some instances of harm to a child may be defined as cultural while in fact other risk factors may be present.

A person who knowingly engages in a practice that is harmful to a child will sometimes use a justification that essentially boils down to "my culture made me do it." For example, I worked with a Puerto Rican woman who counted her daughters' pubic hair, had given them douches since they were infants, and inspected their underarms as she tested out various deodorants. She claimed these practices were common in Puerto Rico, where parents were "affectionate" unlike U.S. parents who were cold and distant. In fact, this behavior would be considered as bizarre and invasive in Puerto Rico as it is on the mainland. . . .

Not the Whole Story

When hearing a justification of a behavior based on culture, it is important to pay attention to who is defining what qualifies as "cultural." As [S.M.] Okin points out [in *Is Multiculturalism Bad for Women?* (1999)], cultures are not homogeneous, and the person who is defining what is "cultural" may be the one who is benefiting from the behavior. Frequently, questionable behaviors that are explained away as cultural are behaviors that oppress or restrict women and children (e.g., the veil, genital cutting, wife beating, corporal punishment). So yes, while it may be true that beating one's children is somewhat more common in Portugal than in the United States, a Portuguese family will nevertheless be required to conform to the law where it resides; and certainly not all families in Portugal beat their children. The family's ethnic or national origin may be *part* of the story, but it is not the whole story.

People who sexually offend are apt to use any and all excuses to justify their behavior, and cultural difference is no exception. Some examples:

- "Someone put a curse [or a hex or an evil eye] on me and I didn't know what I was doing. I was not myself. I was in a trance."

- "In my culture all men break in their daughters. I was teaching her how to please her husband."

- "I was showing my son how to be a man; that's what we do in my country."

- "Back home, it is not unusual for young girls to marry older men. That's why I let my best friend have my daughter."

- "We are very hot-blooded. You put a young girl like my stepdaughter in front of us, dressed the way she was dressed, and we can't control ourselves."

Professionals who are accustomed to working with sex offenders will probably be able to sniff out the most egregious of these justifications. When in doubt, the professional should check with another person from the culture in question (while respecting confidentiality).

Adapting to a New Culture

Sometimes it doesn't matter whether a given practice is culturally acceptable in terms of determining whether abuse has occurred. In the context of Canadian and U.S. law, families may have to abandon certain practices that were tolerated in their countries of origin. When a practice is culturally acceptable in a country of origin but unacceptable in the United States or Canada, children still need to be protected. However, the notion that the practice was acceptable in the country of origin should be taken into account in assessing the family's overall stability and the most appropriate intervention. For example, let's say a Korean family that recently emigrated uses physically abusive corporal punishment with their children, which is common in Korea. Maybe they strike the back of their children's legs with a stick, leaving a mark. It would be entirely appropriate for the parents to have charges of physical abuse substantiated against them. However, if the parents seem amenable to change and did not seem to be aware of the different standards for child raising in their new country, if they do not have other risk factors such as substance abuse or domestic violence, they may not need parenting classes, which are likely to cause them to "lose face," but rather just an occasional contact to make sure they are conforming to the newly learned expectations. It would be important to establish a pathway for the children to seek assistance (e.g., from a school counselor) if the physical abuse recurs.

In other words, the national or ethnic roots of the behavior should be considered relevant in assessing a family and deciding which interventions are most appropriate, but are less apt to be important in determining whether abuse has occurred.

The Effects of
Childhood Abuse Last
Long into Adulthood

Alice Miller

In the following excerpt from her book, The Body Never Lies: The Lingering Effects of Cruelty to Children, *Alice Miller, a psychologist, contends that many adults who were physically and emotionally abused as children tend to deny and minimize the abuse because Western culture normalizes abusive behavior toward children. Arguing that childhood abuse has long-lasting consequences that reach well into adulthood, Miller maintains that in order to obtain "true adulthood," adults who have been abused as children must contend with their repressed emotions and integrate the story of their experience of abuse into their lives instead of denying its influence.*

Born in Poland in 1923, Alice Miller is the author of many books, including Prisoners of Childhood: The Drama of the Gifted Child, For Your Own Good: Hidden Cruelty in Child-Rearing and the Roots of Violence, *and* Thou Shalt Not Be Aware: Society's Betrayal of the Child. *In her practice and her research, Miller maintains that most depressions and other mental illness are caused by emotional and physical maltreatment in childhood.*

In my reading of the notes sent in to the "Our Childhood" forums [on Miller's Web site] over the past few years, one thing has struck me repeatedly. Most newcomers write that, while they have been visiting the forum for some time, they have serious doubts whether they have come to the right place because they themselves never really experienced abuse in childhood. Appalled by the sufferings reported on there, they say that, although they were occasionally beaten and exposed to contempt or other forms of humiliation, they never had to suffer anything remotely like the cruelties inflicted on many of the forum participants. In the course of time, however, these newcomers also start reporting on shocking behavior on the part of their parents, behavior that can be unreservedly classified as abuse and is also considered as such by the others. They need some time to actually feel the suffering they went through as children. Thanks to the sympathy of the other participants, they can gradually admit their true feelings.

A Common Attitude

This phenomenon is a reflection of the attitude displayed by the entire population of the world with regard to child abuse and cruelty to children. Such behavior is at best regarded as an involuntary "lapse from grace," committed by parents who, though they have the best intentions, are simply overtaxed from time to time by the burden of bringing up a child. In the same vein, unemployment or overwork are quoted as the reason that a father gives his children a slap, or marital tensions are cited as the reason a mother has beaten her children with a hanger until it breaks. Such absurd explanations are the fruits of the morality we live by, a system that has always taken the part of the adults and left the children to fend for themselves as best they may. From this perspective, it is of course impossible to perceive the sufferings of children for what they are. It was this realization that prompted me to set up these forums, where people can tell the story of what they have been through and in time, so I hope, reveal what a little child has to go through as long as he or she is deprived of support from society. These reports demonstrate how an extreme form of hatred can evolve. It is so strong that originally innocent children can later, in adulthood, put the insane fantasies of a madman into practice. They can organize, acclaim, support, defend, and finally forget something as monstrous as the Holocaust.

The inquiry into the childhood patterns, the abuse, and the humiliation that have contributed to turning normal children into monsters is still, however, a matter of public neglect. These monsters and the people who have directed their feelings of anger and rage against themselves and have fallen ill for that reason have one thing in common: they ward off any kind of accusation from the parents who once maltreated them so severely. They do not know what that treatment has done to them, they do not know how much they have suffered from it. Above all, they do not want to know. They see it as something beneficial, something inflicted on them for their own good.

Self-therapy manuals and the extensive literature on therapeutic care tell much the same story. Hardly anywhere do we find an author coming out squarely on the side of the child. Readers are advised to "snap out" of the role of victim, to stop blaming others for the things that have gone wrong in their lives, to be true to their own selves. This, they are told, is the only way of freeing themselves from the past and maintaining good relations with their parents. For me, such advice embodies the contradictions of poisonous pedagogy and of conventional morality. It is actively dangerous because it is very likely to leave the former victims in a state of confusion and moral uncertainty, so that the individuals in question may never be able to attain true adulthood throughout their whole lives.

True adulthood would mean no longer denying the truth. It would mean feeling the repressed suffering, consciously acknowledging the story remembered by the body at an emotional level, and integrating that story instead of repressing it. Whether contact with the parents can then in fact be maintained will depend on the given circumstances in each individual case. What is absolutely imperative is the termination of the harmful attachment to the *internalized* parents of childhood, an attachment that, though we call it love, certainly does not deserve the name. It is made up of different ingredients, such as gratitude, compassion, expectations, denial, illusions, obedience, fear, and the anticipation of punishment.

Destructive Dependence

Time and again, I have asked myself why therapy works for some people while others remain the prisoners of their symptoms despite years of analysis or therapeutic care. In each and every case I examined, I was able to establish that when people found the kind of therapeutic care and companionship that enabled them to discover their own story and give free expression to their indignation at their parents' behavior, they were able to liberate themselves from the maltreated child's destructive attachment. As adults they were able to take their lives into their own hands and did not need to hate their parents. The opposite was the case with people whose therapists enjoined them to forgive and forget, actually believing that such forgiveness could have a salutary, curative effect. They remained trapped in the position of small children who believe they love their parents but in fact allow themselves to be controlled all their lives by the internalized parents and ultimately develop some kind of illness that leads to premature death. Such dependency *actively fosters the hatred* that, though repressed, remains active, and it drives them to direct their aggression at innocent people. We only hate as long as we feel totally powerless.

I have received hundreds of letters confirming this assertion. Paula, a twenty-six-year-old woman who suffered from various allergies, wrote saying that every time she visited her uncle when she was still a child he would subject her to sexual harassment, unashamedly fondling her breasts even in the presence of other members of the family. At the same time, this uncle was the only member of the family to pay any attention to the girl. No one protected or defended her. When she complained to her parents, they said she should not let him do it. Instead of standing by her, they foisted the responsibility for the whole affair onto the child. When her uncle fell ill with cancer, Paula refused to visit him because of the fury and disgust the old man now inspired in her. But her therapist was convinced that she would regret this refusal later and that there was no point in arousing the animosity of her family at such a difficult time. It would not do her any good. Accordingly, Paula went to see him, swallowing her genuine feelings of repulsion. Amazingly, when he died, she had a complete change of heart. She actually felt affection for her late uncle. The therapist was satisfied with her, Paula was satisfied with herself: love had triumphed over her hatred and cured her of her allergies. Suddenly, however, she developed severe asthma and she was completely incapable of understanding this new illness. She had purged herself, she had forgiven her uncle and bore no malice against him. So why this punishment? She interpreted the outbreak of the illness as a retribution for her earlier feelings of anger and indignation. Then she read a book of mine, and her illness prompted her to write to me. Her asthma disappeared as soon as she relinquished her "love" for her uncle. It was an example of obedience, not love.

Another woman was astounded by the fact that after years of psychoanalysis she had pains in her legs that no doctor could find an explanation for. In the end, her physicians were forced to admit that the pains might be psychosomatic. In her analytic sessions she had been working for years on the so-called fantasy that she had been sexually abused by her father. More than anything else, she wanted to believe her analyst's version that these were fantasies and not real memories. But all these speculations did nothing to help her understand why she was in such pain. When she finally terminated the treatment, the pains in her legs vanished overnight! They had been a signal that she was living in a world that she could not "step out of." She wanted to run away from her analyst and his mis-guided—and misguiding—interpretations, but she did not dare to. For a time, the pains in her legs were able to block the need to escape, until she made the decision to terminate the analysis and no longer expect any benefit from it.

Leaving Behind Unhealthy Attachment

The attachment to parental figures I am trying to describe here is an attachment to parents who have inflicted injury on their children. It is an attachment that prevents us from help-ing ourselves. The unfulfilled natural needs of the child are later transferred to therapists, partners, or our own children. We cannot believe that those needs were really ignored, or possibly even trampled on by our parents in such a way that we were forced to repress them. We hope that the other people we relate to will finally give us what we have been looking for, understand, support, and respect us, and relieve us of the dif-ficult decisions life brings with it. As these expectations are fostered by the denial of childhood reality, we cannot give them up. As I said earlier, they cannot be relinquished by an act of will. But they will disappear in time if we are deter-mined to face up to our own truth. This is not easy. It is al-most always painful. But it is possible.

In the forums, we frequently observe that some people get annoyed if others in the group respond to the deeds of their parents with indignation, although they do not know the par-ents and although their reaction is based entirely on the ac-count given by the person in question. But it is one thing to complain about one's parents deeds and quite another to take the facts of the matter fully and completely seriously. The lat-ter course arouses the infant's fear of punishment. Accord-ingly, many prefer to leave their earliest perceptions in a state of repression, to avoid looking the truth in the face, to ex-tenuate their parents' deeds, and to reconcile themselves with the idea of forgiveness. But this attitude merely serves to perpetuate the futile expectations we have entertained since our childhood.

I embarked on my first analysis in 1958. Looking back, I have the impression that my analyst was strongly influenced by traditional morality. I was not aware of the fact myself because I had grown up with the same system of values. Of course, this meant that there was no chance for me to discover that I had been abused as a child. To realize that fact I needed a witness who had already made the same discovery herself, someone who no longer shared the customary denial of child abuse that is prevalent in our society. Today, over forty years later, this attitude is still anything but self-evident. Reports by therapists claiming to be on the children's side normally betray a "corrective" attitude they are completely unaware of because they have never reflected on the fact. Although many such therapists quote from my books and encourage their clients to do justice to themselves, rather than adapt and adjust to the demands made on them by others, I myself as a reader of their reports have the feeling that the advice they mete out is in fact advice that cannot genuinely be followed. What I describe as the result of a personal history is treated like some kind of character flaw that needs to be corrected. We are told to respect ourselves, to estimate our own qualities, and all kinds of other things. There is a whole repertory of injunctions designed to help people to regain their self-esteem. But the barriers in their minds are resistant to these injunctions. As I see it, the point is that people who cannot estimate and respect themselves, who cannot allow themselves the free expression of their creativity, do not do so voluntarily. These barriers are the result of each person's individual story. They want to understand how they have become that way, then they need to know that story as precisely as possible and need to engage with it emotionally. Once they have understood this fact, and are actually able to feel the implications of the story (not just grasp them intellectually), then they will need no more advice. What these adults need then is an enlightened witness who can accompany them on the road to their own truth, help them embark on a process in the course of which they will finally permit themselves the always-wanted but always-denied things: trust, respect, and love for themselves. We must abandon the expectation that someday the parents will give us what they withheld in childhood.

Acknowledging and Overcoming Denial

This is the reason so few people have actually taken that road, why so many content themselves with the advice of their therapists or let religious notions prevent them from discovering their own truth. Earlier on, I suggested that fear is the decisive factor in all this. But I also believe that this fear will be reduced when the facts of childhood abuse are no longer treated as a taboo in our society. So far, the victims of such abuse have denied its existence because of the infant fear that lives on inside them. In this way they have contributed to the all-pervasive denial of the truth. But once the former victims begin to reveal what happened to them, then therapists too will be forced to acknowledge these realities. A short while ago, a well-known German psychoanalyst stated publicly that he rarely encountered former victims of childhood abuse in his practice. This is an astounding statement, because I know of literally no one who suffers from psychic symptoms and seeks treatment for them without having at least been beaten and humiliated in childhood. I call such treatment abuse, although for thousands of years it has been regarded as a legitimate parenting method. It may be no more than a question of definition, but in this case the definition is decisive.

CONTEMPORARY
ISSUES
COMPANION

CHAPTER 3

Victims of Child Abuse Tell Their Stories

I Never Told Anyone I Was Molested

Jake Cooney

In the following viewpoint, Jake Cooney explains why he never told anyone about how he and his brother were molested as children by a neighbor. As a teenager and an adult, he tried very hard to forget what had happened because he felt ashamed. When he learned as an adult that his neighbor had died, he had a flood of memories, but it was not until he read about the sex scandals in the Catholic Church in 2001 that the memory surfaced again, and he decided to tell his story to Newsweek. *As a child, he did not think he was allowed to tell his story, but now, he writes, "I choose not to be silent."*

Jake Cooney lives in New York City. He has written first-person pieces for the New York Observer, Newsday, *and* NY Press *magazine.*

"Ed Kell died," my mother said.

"What?" I said.

"He fell back over his porch."

"Fell back?"

"He was drunk," she said.

That was 14 years ago—the last time I thought about him until the Roman Catholic Church scandal broke in 2001 and I found myself wondering why the victims had waited so long to tell anyone. I never stopped to ask myself the same question. I didn't yet realize that they were just like me: they had been used by someone they looked up to and were too ashamed to admit it, even to themselves.

My older brother Mike (no real names are used) and I were "Irish twins," born 10 months apart. We grew up on a dead end four blocks from where Ed Kell lived in a blue-collar, predominantly Catholic suburb an hour west of Boston.

Being around Ed—a former [Green Bay] Packers draft pick—was like walking on an active volcano. Whoever was foolish enough to argue with him, or wasn't white, Irish or Catholic, became his prey, but the times he was nice to you made you feel as if you'd won an award. He was just a self-appointed neighborhood coach, but to us he was superhuman, and he would demonstrate this by reverse-curling hundreds of pounds or crushing bottle caps between his fingers.

Special Attention

The day before it happened, I was shooting free throws at Mr. Johnson's when Ed came down the road. "Heard you sprained your ankle," he said.

"Yeah, but the doctor said it's almost better," I said, turning the ball in my hands.

"Doctors don't know jack," he said. "Come by tomorrow. I'll check the muscle tone like I did for your brother."

The next day I walked to Ed's house. He seemed nervous. Without any small talk he nodded to the door of a room. "I'll be in in a minute. Take off your sneakers and socks." I did what he said and waited. He walked in smoking his cigarette, pulled a chair in front of me and, speaking lower than usual, said, "Let's have a look."

He looked at my sprained right ankle and compared it with the left. Then he said, "Stand up." He touched them both, mumbling about swelling and ligaments, then told me to roll my pants up to my knees so he could look for signs I was favoring it. When I did he said, "No, you're gonna have to take 'em off. I need to look at the rest of your leg." I was in

113

shock, but with the notion of being at the doctor's—awkward but necessary—I took them off.

As I walked home, I kept remembering his hands shaking as he said, "Take down your underwear." It all came flooding back to me—the day my mother saw Ed going through Mike's underwear drawer and he claimed he was only looking at his posters, and another time when she saw him talking to Mike in his bedroom. It hit me—I'd been molested.

I Hated Myself More than Him

When I got home, I took the basketball outside and started punching it until I was on the verge of tears. I thought, what if he comes over now looking for more? I'll throw this ball at his head, then get the hammer from the garage and tear into him with the hooked end. Sure enough, a couple of hours later he came by. "How's it going?" he said, leaning out his car window. I didn't answer. "Your brother home?"

"No."

"All right, tell him I dropped by," he said as he eased the car down the street.

I hadn't even raised my voice. I stood there, hating myself even more than I hated him. Telling my parents would only make the nightmare real. I wasn't trying to stop Ed Kell or even avenge my brother—if it had happened to him he wouldn't want to talk about it, either. I was trying to forget.

The next time I thought about it was a couple of years later, when I heard a state trooper came home and caught Ed molesting his son. There was no exposure—just the officer and his friends beating Ed unconscious.

No Shame in Telling

Ed's death made me face, as an adult, what had happened, but I needed 14 more years of forgetting and months of reading about the church scandal before the memory surfaced again. For all those years I was either in denial or too ashamed to tell. If I had, maybe it never would have happened to the state trooper's son. Maybe my brother and I wouldn't have waited 20 years to talk about it.

As Tim Robbins accepted his Oscar . . . for playing an abuse victim in "Mystic River," he told all victims that "there is no shame" in telling. As a 13-year-old, I didn't realize I had a choice, but as an adult, I do. I choose not to be ashamed anymore. I choose not to be silent.

I Blamed Myself for My Adoptive Father's Abuse

Mary Black Bonnet

In the following viewpoint, Mary Black Bonnet, a Native American, explains that because their birth parents could not take care of them, Mary and her older sister, Margaret, were placed into foster care and adopted by a white family. As Mary relates, her adoptive father was prone to violence, bullying the neighbors and beating his children. He molested Mary until her adoptive mother divorced him. Black Bonnet writes, "The only memories I have of my childhood are ones that include abuse, rape and violence. I know that I lived my life without any sense of safety. I remember praying that I would make it to see the next day, alive, and in one piece." As an adult, Black Bonnet connects the abuse she suffered as a child at the hands of white adoptive parents with the history of the abuse Native Americans suffered as a conquered people.

Mary Black Bonnet is a full-blooded member of the Sicangu Lakota tribe from the Rosebud Reservation in South Dakota. She is currently a student at the University of South Dakota at Vermillion. Upon graduation, she plans to teach writing at universities and schools on reservations. Her work has been published in Nagi-Ho Journal *and* Genocide of the Mind: New Native American Writing.

He'd come into my bedroom at night and would crawl into bed with me. It was late, and I'd been sleeping for a while, but it wouldn't matter, because as soon as I heard him coming, I'd jolt awake. My heart would pound, and I'd start to shake—terrified. I knew what was going to happen. At first all

Mary Black Bonnet, "In Search of Mother Turtle," *Frontiers,* vol. 23, 2002, pp. 43–53.

he did was kiss me and penetrate me with his finger. But this hurt, and I'd leave my body to escape the pain he'd inflict and the fear that consumed me. I'd imagine I was talking to my birthmother or maybe my adoptive mom. I only knew I couldn't be there in that room with him, and it's probably what saved me from going crazy. When he'd finish and go back to his room, I'd return but lay awake for hours, scared. What if he came back? Sometimes he did, sometimes he didn't. Between the ages of five and eight this was a nightly ritual. It happened without fail. I also knew there was nothing I could do to stop it, and there wasn't anyone who would stop him from doing it again.

He never spoke to me when he'd do this, except to say before he left, "Don't say anything about this to anyone, or people will know how bad you are." Or he'd say, "Don't say anything about this or Mom and Margaret will die, and it will be all your fault." That was enough to keep my mouth shut. For one thing, I truly believed that my adoptive dad was capable of killing, but more importantly, Mom and [my sister] Margaret were my saviors. In front of them he could always hit me, but he could never hurt me sexually. I also felt that what he was doing was wrong, and if I was going to get in trouble for it, I decided I must have done something to provoke it. I walked around with guilt oozing from my skin, and that is what made it so easy for him to pin all the guilt on an innocent six-year-old Lakota girl from the Rosebud Sioux Reservation. . . .

Recurring Nightmares

The abuse went on until I was ten. He had told us children that he was moving to Texas, and to me, from Nebraska to Texas was the other side of the country. So, two days after he told us he was leaving, and I thought he'd be far enough away, I told my adoptive mom. She leapt into action, grabbing me from my bed and dragging me to my sister's room. I didn't know what was going on exactly, except that my adoptive mom was mad for quite a few days. She spoke on the phone a lot, usually after I'd gone to bed. But, I really didn't care. I just knew then that he could not see us anymore, and that meant he couldn't hurt me anymore. This time it was for real, and that was all I cared about. I tried to go on with my life. I acted as if everything was normal and that I would never be bothered by it again.

But I was. I had nightmares about him coming to school and taking me away, not allowing me to see my adoptive mom or my sister. In the dreams he was really mad and very mean. I heard his voice in my head telling me that if he found out I had told, he'd be really mad at me and make me sorry I said anything. I was scared and wanted to talk to my adoptive mom about it. However, when I brought it up one day, she told me, "Forget about it. That part of your life is over now." The tone in her voice made me ashamed for asking about it. So I dropped it and never brought it up again. What I didn't realize at the time was that it was her own guilt and discomfort she didn't want to face. That has to be a huge burden. But, as usual, I took her comment to mean I was wrong for speaking of it, and of thinking of it. So, I did what I had always done, I buried it deep in the back of my mind and told myself it didn't happen and that I was fine. Though, because it did happen, its repercussions have affected my life for many years.

It took me many years to heal and become healthy. I suffered many effects that come from being an abuse victim. I hated my body, feared men, was self-conscious, nervous, eager to please, and self-abusive. I developed a horrible need to be perfect, and when I didn't measure up to my own standards, as well as those from my family, I'd hurt myself. At first it was little things, hitting myself in the face, pulling my own hair, biting myself, but as the years passed and I got older, the way I hurt myself grew in intensity. I started cutting myself. Because I'd stuffed my feelings of the abuse deep inside, when I'd get upset, I would feel as if I couldn't breathe. So, I'd cut myself. I wouldn't initially feel the cut, but as soon as it started bleeding, I would be able to breathe again. I didn't know it was called self-mutilation at the time, it was just something I had done to cope. Though it was unhealthy, it helped me deal with my life when it got too crazy. I didn't hate myself enough to want to commit suicide, but just enough to make myself suffer for my imperfections. As the years went by, I began to cut deeper and leave lasting scars. I scared myself once. I sliced my vein, it bled and bled and I couldn't get it to stop. I was afraid I was going to bleed to death. I couldn't tell anyone because no one knew I was cutting myself, and I feared that if I told anyone, I'd be seen as crazy or unstable, which was my worst fear. I fought every day to appear normal, healthy, and well adjusted to those around me. And when people would say things like, "You have a good head on your shoulders," I would be happy that I was able to pull off such an appearance.

Years of Feeling Worthless

My adoptive mom had remarried by the time I was twelve, and my new stepfather was the complete opposite of my adoptive father, yet in some ways he mirrored him. He didn't talk to us or hug us; he wouldn't even touch us. But for a twelve-year-old girl who was desperate to be given some kind of warmth and affection, this was, in some ways, worse than the abuse I had experienced at the hands of my adoptive father. My stepfather's indifference and complete lack of affection confirmed my unspoken hidden fear—I was dirty, bad, and unworthy of love.

I spent years believing I was worthless and nothing. However, I finally went into counseling when I was fifteen. It was a long, hard journey, and I sometimes dropped out because it got too hard. Having buried the memories of the abuse so deep, I was in no hurry to dredge up the unpleasantness of my experience. I finally realized that if I wanted to get better, if I wanted to feel good about myself and have healthy relationships, I would have to stay in counseling and talk about the horrible things I had locked away for years. No one could do it for me, and I wasn't going to be complete until I did. I knew I wanted to have children and get married someday, but in order to do that I had to get my life together and learn not just to like myself, but to love myself for who I was and what I had come through.

My best friend at the time was attending Alcoholics Anonymous meetings for her alcohol problem and told me once that I could not love anyone else until I loved myself. When she said that I realized it was true, and if I continued down this self-destructive path, I was never going to be healthy enough to have children or a marriage. If I continued as I had been up to that point, I would end up in an unhealthy, dysfunctional relationship similar to those that surrounded me all my life. Having seen and felt the effects of what a dysfunctional marriage can do to children, I did not want that for my children. I knew when I got to the point of having my own children, I didn't want them to ever have to know what it felt like to be lonely and isolated, ashamed of both who you were as well as where you came from. In order to do that, I would have to break the cycle of abuse from which I came. I had to learn to love myself enough and realize that I was worth something, and that I would become someone in this great world. I had been kept alive for this long, had come through all these life altering experiences, the Great Spirit must have had a greater purpose for me. It took me a long time to learn and finally believe that. After many years of counseling and a strong desire to get better, day by day, I got closer to achieving that goal. I still suffered from self-doubt, a desire to please everyone, and episodes of self-mutilation, but these became less frequent. My relationships with others got better as did my relationships with men. I finally grew comfortable in my own skin and eventually even proud of who I had become and what I had to come through to get there. . . .

Surviving Against the Odds

My life is not much different from the history of what the Lakota people went through. White men have been raping Indian women for years. Their quest was to conquer the earth, control it. Hundreds of children were taken from their birth families and placed in white foster homes. The government felt that this would make us all a little less Indian. In 1879, Captain Richard Henry Pratt founded the Carlisle Indian School and assigned it a motto, "Kill the Indian. Save the man." The goal of the Carlisle Indian School was to do exactly that, "de-Indianize" the children. What they didn't realize is that when you are born an Indian, you die an Indian. No one can ever take that from us. I believe that no matter where we grew up, we have instilled in us immense spirit. It's the spirit that keeps you going when you would rather die, when you think it would be easier to just give up and let things be. Most of all, it's about surviving. In the Lakota language we say "Ta-kini," which means "survivor." My people have been surviving for years despite all odds. You have to keep fighting to succeed, and for no other reason than to prove it to yourself.

My Mother Did Not Protect Me from My Stepfather's Beatings

Daryl T. Moore

In the personal narrative that follows, Daryl T. Moore, a freelance writer who lives in Tallahassee, Florida, describes how, as a small child, he struggled to find a way to keep his drunken stepfather from beating him. He describes the humiliation and anger he felt as a child, along with feelings of anger and abandonment because his mother did not protect him from the abuse. As a young adult, Moore writes, he had many difficulties with intimacy and feeling trusting and safe in relationships with women. It was not until he finally confronted his mother about his childhood abuse and his mother tearfully apologized, he says, that he was able to forgive her. He hopes that understanding his feelings about his childhood abuse will help him be successful in his adult relationships.

I had already been struck by my stepfather's mahogany cane several times, but I kept going back. I was playing in the front yard outside our old duplex when I heard him call me that day. It was pretty stupid of me to climb those stairs every time he called—especially knowing how drunk he was. But when you're 8 years old, you don't make the wisest decisions.

At the top of the stairs I pushed open the door of our unit and saw him standing in the living room with a liquor bottle in one hand and his mahogany cane in the other, his country-music records blasting. He asked me whether or not I had disobeyed him. I had not, in fact, committed the deed in question and proceeded to tell him so. That's when my stepfather hit me with the mahogany cane—again and again—until I lost count.

The rest is blurred. But after a while, I was back downstairs, crying profusely and wiping tears from my eyes. I was badly bruised on my head, arms and legs, but at least it was over now—or so I thought: In fact, there would be a replay. Again he called me upstairs to answer his question; when I responded, down came the cane on my head. I began to hate and fear that mahogany cane as much as I feared my stepfather.

Lying to Avoid the Beatings

The third time he called I was terrified. Instead of bounding up the stairs as I had done the first two times, I now crawled up slowly, hoping to delay the cane as long as possible. Once I reached the top, predictably, the same fate awaited me. Naively I continued to subject myself to this horror for the next two hours or so—until I got smart and lied. I told him I had done it.

Then he let me play downstairs for the rest of the afternoon. Though this was not the first or last such incident I endured, it stood out as one of the worst. I'll remember it all my life. When my mom returned home, she tended to my wounds—three or four bumps on my head, a dozen bruises and marks all over my body. This became the routine in our house for the next few years. It didn't occur to me then that my mom's refusal to get me away from her abusive husband was bad. However, by my teenage years I began to question her role.

In college I had read about women who stayed with husbands who beat them, but most of them left when the abusive man started on their child; their love for their children was greater than their love for themselves. My mom was never beaten by my stepfather, which seemed good enough for her, even though he ravaged me mercilessly. I began to doubt her affection. Didn't she love me? Why didn't she leave and take

123

me with her? Why did she let me endure such pain? Why didn't she save me?

Fears of Abandonment

I felt abandoned by my mother, and ultimately fear of abandonment transferred over to any other woman who claimed to love me. I was afraid of committed relationships. I had a series of girlfriends whom I always suspected of cheating, though they had shown no signs of infidelity. I accused them of not loving me, though they had broken their backs to show me otherwise.

My dysfunctional relationships continued until I confronted my mother about my childhood abuse. I'd held a grudge bordering on hatred against her for many years. Hurt and pain filled her eyes, and she was visibly broken, whispering, "I'm sorry." She told me she had been naive and stupid and would do anything to turn back time so she could spare me pain. But my feelings didn't really change until she said, "I love you." My heart melted. I was overjoyed, realizing that I wasn't abandoned. My mother did love me. Forgiving her was my first step toward opening myself to the love of other women.

Since then, I have a renewed outlook on my relationships with women. I've learned to be committed, to trust and to share love. I've learned to be a strong Black man and a child-abuse survivor rather than a victim. That way, I break the cane, the cane doesn't break me.

My Disabled Daughter Was a Victim of Abuse

Doreen Williams, interviewed by Anne McDowall

In the following article, Anne McDowall, director of family services at the National Deaf Children's Society in England, notes that disabled children are three times more likely to be abused or neglected than other children but that very little work has been done to protect disabled children. In the United Kingdom, she writes, the Council for Disabled Children and the National Society for the Prevention of Cruelty to Children have formed a Working Group on Child Abuse and Disability to better protect disabled children and adults. McDowall shares the story of Doreen Williams, the mother of a developmentally disabled young woman who lives in a group home. A volunteer had been molesting her daughter Alice for at least a year, but Alice was too frightened to tell. The abuse eventually became known when Alice injured herself as the volunteer was assaulting her. Although the volunteer was sentenced to four-and-a-half years in prison, Doreen Williams still worries how to keep Alice, a little girl in a young woman's body, safe.

Disabled children are three times more likely to be abused or neglected than able-bodied children, according to the most recent major study of this subject, which was done in the United States. Three times more. This should ring alarm bells right through our Departments of Health and Education and all the policy-making quangos [quasi-nongovernmental organizations], but it isn't.

Rarely are disabled children more than a footnote in important guidance papers.

Anne McDowall, "Comment & Analysis: Public Voices: 'I Mustn't Tell Anyone. But He Did Hurt Me Mum': This Week, Part Two of Our Series Where People Working in Child Protection Tell Us How It Is. Today, Abuse of the Disabled," *The Guardian*, January 14, 2003. Copyright © 2003 by Anne McDowall. Reproduced by permission.

The Department of Health does not require child protection registers to identify whether children they list have disabilities. If this was done, at least we'd know how many are on the register, in what way they were abused and what action was taken. There also needs to be a major piece of research, equivalent to that in the US.

Another problem is that if children can't speak for themselves—using oral speech—they're not seen as credible witnesses.

The Council for Disabled Children and the NSPCC [National Society for the Prevention of Cruelty to Children] have convened a new body, the National Working Group on Child Abuse and Disability, bringing together a range of people with experience of the issues and a will to do something about them. My hope is that this group will achieve recognition at the highest levels and will stimulate change in the legal and care systems, as well as properly funded research.

Doreen's Story

Doreen Williams [tells about] the abuse of her stepdaughter, an adult with the mental age of a child. All names are fictitious save those of Mrs Williams and the care volunteer now in jail for her daughter's rape, William 'Keith' Isaac:

Our daughter Alice was living in a small residential home for people with learning disabilities, run by Stockport social services. The workers in the home were lovely.

Every week or two a volunteer, Keith Isaac, collected Alice and another resident, Brian, to take them swimming. In the minibus, Isaac also brought his son, Matthew, who had Down's syndrome and lived with his parents; Alice called Matthew her boyfriend.

Keith Isaac was in his 60s. Before retiring, he'd been a care worker with mentally disabled people for years for Stockport social services. He kept in this line of activity as a Mencap charity volunteer—he was actually vice-president of the Stockport branch. Taking the group swimming was part of his volunteer work. I said I didn't like the idea of a man taking handicapped ladies swimming; like a six-year-old, Alice would think nothing of walking out wearing nothing. Her IQ is under 50. But the social services say these volunteers are few and far between and you have to be very grateful.

After swimming, Isaac used to drop his son at home. Then he would drive with the others to the Gateway Club, which is a social club where they all had discos and things. He'd lock Brian in the minibus and tell him to clean it, while he'd take Alice and Grace—another woman they took swimming—into the club, and that's when the rapes would take place.

We think it went on for at least a year. Isaac admitted to five [instances of intercourse with Alice]. We're sure it was more. She said if she had period on, he'd make her do other things and give her a sweet to get rid of the nasty taste. By that, you knew it was more than five times.

I've asked Alice why she didn't tell us. She said: 'He told me that if I told a soul, then he would not let me see Matthew again. I love Matthew, and I want to see Matthew. That is why I mustn't tell anyone.' But, she said, he did hurt me, mum.

The only reason it ever came out is because Alice fell and hit her head. When she reported that, there were questions. Then it emerged what he'd been doing. It was horrendous.

All of a sudden Alice had a social worker, from out of the sky! And of course it snowballed from there.

Everybody knew, except us. It wasn't till nine days later that we got a phone call, but with very little information. Social services said Alice had said: 'Don't tell mum and dad.' The main people in charge at social services wouldn't return our calls.

A Child in an Adult's Body

But once the police were in touch they were brilliant. Neil Hewitt, the detective constable doing the investigation, he

127

would ring and keep us informed. But social services? Nothing. I haven't had one letter or one phone call from any of the management before or since the court case [in March 2002 where Isaac was sentenced to four-and-a-half years by Manchester crown court].

I want Alice to be her age, I don't want her to be a little girl. But mentally she is a little girl. How should she be treated: as an adult or a child? One thing I would say is that in the residential homes or going out on trips, carers or escorts should always be in pairs, because even with thorough checks, people are bound to slip through the net.

This Keith Isaac, he had no record. Talking about him, someone who used to work for Stockport social services said: 'He was so respected, he did so much good work.'

What do you say? Yes, great work in the Gateway Club, didn't he, with my daughter.

Seeking Closure for Memories of Past Abuse

Heather Howdle

In the following essay, Heather Howdle reflects that even though she has a successful career and happy family life, her memories of childhood abuse by her father grew stronger as her own children approached the age she was when she was first abused. Even though the abuse had occurred thirty-five years ago, Howdle decided that she needed to seek closure on her own experience of abuse in order to be a better parent. Working with a therapist, Howdle decided to discuss the abuse with her family. Because her father denied the abuse and her mother and siblings expressed more concern for his standing in the community than for the harm he had done to her, Howdle decided to press criminal charges. Although she found the legal system a little intimidating, in making her story public, Howdle writes, she felt that she was able to protect others from being abused and to find peace for herself in the present, placing her abuse in the past. Howdle offers advice to other survivors who might be contemplating filing criminal charges. Heather Howdle is a physiotherapist who lives in Winnipeg, Manitoba.

Why talk about this now? Why is it important to try to have justice 35 years after the abuse began? It is because surviving physically is not enough. It is because the worst damage is emotional: the horror lives on in the problems it causes after the physical abuse stops.

As a child, I was led to believe that the abuse I was subjected to was normal. But it didn't feel right or comfortable. Later, I began to understand that what I had gone through was not just unpleasant, not just abnormal, but a criminal offence. It came as a shock to know that someone I loved and trusted, someone in a position of authority and protection, would do this.

A Double Life

Living with memories of abuse is like living a double life. I had begun to gather external success in my life as a physiotherapist, professor and administrator. However, I felt continually doubtful, uncertain and lost. I shut myself off and avoided close relationships. Any time I had a spare moment, my mind would be flooded with memories of the abuse. I made sure that I never had any free time: I drove myself to exhaustion day after day, trying to stay too busy to think about what I was feeling.

Eventually, the sheer volume of activity wasn't enough to repress the memories. I began to find it difficult to accomplish any one thing. I knew I needed help, but I also believed I couldn't trust anyone. I had not been protected by my family members, so how could I trust other people to help me?

When my two children began to approach the age I had been when the abuse began, my memories became stronger and stronger and it was no longer possible to avoid them. I began the long journey towards healing the damaging patterns that the abuse had left in my life. With the help of a good therapist, I learned how to take care of myself and how to connect with my emotions (good and bad) in healthy ways. I learned that taking care of myself was an important first step in the healing process. Eventually, I was able to focus on the positives in my present life and I came to believe that there can be a good life after abuse. I was able to break free of past addictions and began to enjoy my free time.

Yet something was missing—feeling better was not enough. I also wanted to protect other children from being harmed. Seeking justice was necessary for this, and to enable me to put closure on the abuse.

At first I tried mediation with my parents—I thought that it would be best for my family. But it failed. My father denied and minimized the abuse. My mother and a few of my siblings expressed sympathy; however, their main concern seemed to be how my disclosure would affect my father and the family's reputation in the community.

Seeking Closure

Their response triggered something. For the first time, I allowed myself to feel real anger on my own behalf. What had happened to me was wrong. The fact that 35 years had passed did not make it less wrong. I decided to proceed with criminal charges.

At first, the experience was everything I was afraid it would be. A majority of family members closed ranks against me. Some of those who knew about the abuse denied their knowledge when the police questioned them. This was something I had not expected. I later learned that family members often deny the crime rather than admit that they were unwilling (or unable) to stop it. Family members and even friends can be unpredictable and their emotional support and testimony cannot always be counted on.

My advice to survivors is to make sure you have a strong support network before you get involved in the justice system. My support came from my partner, my children, friends and colleagues, as well as the community at large. Here, there was no blaming the victim. When I made my first statement to the police, it gave me an incredible feeling to know that others were behind me. This was crucial during the times I felt pressure from family members to continue pretending that what happened to me was really "nothing." It also helped me a great deal to find a mentor—a friend whose partner was also a sexual abuse survivor and had been through the justice system. He told me what to expect and supported me through the process.

I would advise other survivors to seek civil and criminal advice from a lawyer early on, regardless of whether you decide to proceed. (Legal Aid is an option if you can't afford a lawyer.) In my own case, the statute of limitations on civil damages expired before I knew the cut-off existed. Although there is no time limit on criminal charges in abuse cases, the limit for seeking civil damages is, in most cases, six years from the date you first become aware that abuse has resulted in damage. Talking to a lawyer can help you understand the criminal offences as well as the requirements for a civil suit, in which financial damages can be sought even if there has not been a criminal conviction. It also helps to understand what the law says about clarity, consistency and evidence in case you decide to make a complaint.

Despite the weaknesses of the criminal justice system, I felt the scales of justice tip in my favour when I applied to have the publication ban lifted. My abuser could no longer continue to hide.

Finding Peace

Abusers thrive on silence; they count on it in order to perpetuate their behavior. They convince their victims from an early age that they are 'special' or that there is nothing wrong with what they are doing. And they count on their victims feeling embarrassed and to blame if others find out. For me, being publicly identified as a victim of a crime was a way to become a powerful survivor rather than a victim. I believe that it also helped put the responsibility for the abuse where it belonged: on the abuser. It can also be a warning to others in the community with children.

When I started to tell my story, I finally began to find peace. The outpouring of support has restored my faith in humankind and allowed me to continue the healing process. With the healing came the ability to distance myself emotionally from the painful memories: the abuse has become an external fact and I can live in the present.

Some people said to me that they were not strong enough to tell their stories to police or in a courtroom. For me, strength is not what it took. It was knowing that in telling my story, I might be able to protect others from being abused. Because of this, I feel that, regardless of the final outcome, I would still feel that I gained strength and self-respect in the process.

Preventing Child Abuse

The Foster Care System Can Help Neglected Children

Dawn Turner Trice

In recounting the case study of five young brothers who made national headlines in 1994 when they were removed—along with fourteen other children—from a squalid Chicago apartment, Dawn Turner Trice tells a bigger story about the ways in which foster families can help abused and neglected children heal. Neglected, exposed to drug abuse, and living in filth prior to being placed in foster care, the five Melton brothers have made good progress toward recovery, Trice writes, under the care of their foster mother, Claudine Christian, who provides a consistent structured family environment supported by love and patience.

Dawn Turner Trice is an editor at the Chicago Tribune *and writes for the* Tribune *and National Public Radio's "Morning Edition." The author of two novels, she lives outside Chicago with her husband and daughter.*

When the five brothers arrived at Claudine Christian's farm nearly 10 years ago, they weren't accustomed to having meals at a dining room table and they ate with their fingers.

For the first several nights, they slept in a huddle on the bedroom floor despite brand-new bunk beds purchased just for them. Nightmares crowded their dreams.

The brothers were five of 19 children Chicago police found in February 1994, in a squalid two-bedroom apartment at 219 N. Keystone Ave.

At the time, the Keystone Kids, as they would become known, made national news as one of the country's most disturbing cases of child neglect. Six mothers, five of whom were sisters, collected more than $4,500 a month in welfare checks and food stamps while young children slept on stained mattresses on the floor, waded through mounds of filth and depended on the older children to raise them.

Nearly all of the Keystone children—the original 19 eventually rose to 28 because some of the children weren't in the apartment that night—have either been adopted or have "aged out" of the child welfare system.

According to the Illinois Department of Children and Family Services [DCFS], the five brothers, who now range in age from 12 to 19, are among the last remaining in foster care. Only one other, an 18-year-old, continues to be a ward of the state.

Defying the Odds

In Christian's home, the brothers have defied what most child-welfare experts say is the lot for children who begin their lives under such horrific neglect. They are junior deacons in their small church. While the older boys once had abysmal school attendance, they now miss very few days of school. With Christian, they have chores and boundaries and distinct expectations. They also have frequent contact with their birth mother.

"When everything happened, we were tired of the cameras flashing and everybody knowing our business," says Johnnie Melton, 18. "We were ashamed. But there wasn't any of that here at Mama's house. She took us in and suddenly we had a real home."

Still, Christian, who has been their most ardent advocate, fears they may not have gotten all they need. Despite many successes, the young men struggle in school with behavioral and academic challenges. The oldest has graduated from high school but can barely read.

From the beginning, social workers knew that the children had experienced such profound deprivation that it was going to be difficult to place them in homes individually, let alone as a group.

When Christian agreed to care for the boys for three months until their mother was released from jail, she wasn't prepared for what was coming: The boys fought incessantly and destroyed items in the home. Her husband decided he couldn't take it anymore and moved out. The foster care placement itself would last more than 10 years.

"Before there was a system, there was a tradition," says Christian, 59, who raised five children of her own before the brothers came. "This was our history: If you knew somebody who couldn't raise their babies, then somebody who could stepped forward. This is just what family and neighbors did for one another."

Christian says she couldn't afford to adopt the brothers, but as they wound their way into her heart, despite the difficulties, neither could she imagine letting them go.

A New Chance

A sky-blue ranch house with a white picket fence sits at the foot of a dirt road in the eastern portion of Hopkins Park.

To ward off cold, the front entrance is draped in opaque painter's plastic. A side driveway is unpaved and leads to a worn mini-van and a back yard filled with pens of animals— pigs, horses, rabbits, peacocks—and a basketball court. . . .

The four-bedroom house is modest and immaculate. The kitchen counters are clear and the sink is empty. The carpets display fresh vacuum lines. The way of life here is miles from what the children were accustomed to in the $300-a-month, first-floor apartment on North Keystone Avenue.

On the night police entered the apartment investigating a possible drug sale, they found the 19 children, most of them siblings and first cousins, living amid the stench of soiled diapers, discarded pieces of food and mounds of dirty clothes.

They found a bathroom toilet clogged with waste and tissue paper; roaches that crawled in and out of bags of flour and rotting spaghetti. A 14-year-old boy, who weighed close to 300 pounds, was using a snow shovel in a futile effort to scoop up the mess and make the apartment presentable.

All the children were taken into DCFS custody. The adults were arrested and everyone was released on bond except for the boys' mother, Maxine Melton, whose arrest violated her probation for a previous conviction.

Faced with a 3-year sentence, Melton asked Christian, a longtime friend of the family, to care for her sons until she was released. With time served, Melton expected to be released within a few months, then she would drive out to Christian's 20-acre farm to get her sons.

The boys' fathers—each child has a different one—were either in jail or nowhere to be found.

Chaos Accompanies Foster Children

On Keystone Avenue, the brothers' lives were filled with chaos. And, naturally, chaos followed them to the Christian home.

After Christian and her husband decided to take temporary custody of the boys—who were 2, 5, 6, 8 and 9 years old—social workers began driving them out for visits. Christian got a preview of what life was about to be like. One day the brothers were assembled in the back seat of a social worker's car.

"They were so bad that Anthony [Melton] sat in the back seat dabbing bubble gum into the social worker's hair. When she got here, I had to cut gum out of her hair."

In June 1994, the boys moved in.

They were clean, but they wore secondhand clothes that didn't fit. "They looked like ragamuffins," Christian says. "I went out and immediately bought them some new clothes."

Despite having new bunk beds, they slept together in the center of their bedroom floor wrapped in a comforter with a patchwork design of horses. Sleep was uneven and fitful, broken by nightmares.

"They would wake up in the middle of the night, and I would run into their room and I would grab two or three at a time and just hold them and rock them until they could sleep again. I would say, 'I love you. I love you. I love you.' You just say it until it sticks. You can't play with those words when it comes to the hearts of children. You have to mean it and know it for yourself."

Dealing with Depression and Anger

Still, the children were often depressed and withdrawn. One child constantly destroyed his toys. They busted out windows in the house and tore down an outdoor gazebo. They fought.

Claudell adopted the familiar role of parent, yelling at his brothers trying to keep them in line, fearful that they would be sent away and separated.

"I had to assure him I was there for them until their mother came back," Christian says.

But the workload was overwhelming.

"Some nights my fingers would be raw and bleeding from the work and I was angry and I would be crying and I'd say to my daughter, 'I can't do this.' And she would say: 'Look at them, Ma. Where would they go?'"

Christian says her husband couldn't handle the pressure. The marriage, a second for both, was shaky before the brothers arrived, and soon he asked her to choose between him and the children. She chose the boys. . . .

Family Structure Helps Recovery

At the Christian home, the brothers were given structure and boundaries for the first time in their lives. Christian began taking them to church. One by one they were baptized. Two weeks after arriving they started calling her "Mama." She quit her job as a nursing assistant so she could be with them full time and now supports them with the $2,500 check the boys receive each month because they are state wards.

As Christian began to spend more time with the boys, she noticed disturbing behavior. They would take baking soda—sometimes baby powder or laundry detergent—and spread it across the table, then use a butter knife to divide it into lines, mimicking adults they had seen using drugs. . . .

Claudell, who often tried to keep his siblings in line, was at once helpful and given to intense bouts of anger and depression.

"I was so used to taking care of so many kids," Claudell says. "That was my job, but I just couldn't do it for myself."

Claudell's sorrow seemed bottomless and his behavior was so poor at school that he was placed in a special class, then a special school for children with behavior problems.

"They all have bruised spirits, but him being the oldest, he was so much more worse off," Christian says. "It breaks your heart because it makes you know that sometimes when you come from such a start, no amount of counseling or therapy or love can turn things around."

She says she has told him he will always have a home with her.

"He knows I mean this from the bottom of my heart," she says, nodding. "He knows he always has a home."

A Chance to Be Kids

A dense fog hangs over the cornfields like an old knotty blanket. Along Main Street, you can barely see the green sign that says "Hopkins Park, population 800," or the shuttered businesses and houses, many of which are pushed back from the street.

From this perspective, you would hardly know that Hopkins Park—about two hours south of downtown Chicago in

Kankakee County—sits in one of the poorest, most geographically isolated townships in the country. Many of the roads here are dirt or gravel. For some, indoor plumbing, natural gas lines, safe drinking water and transportation are luxuries.

A few miles from Main Street, a school bus bumps along a dirt road and stops at the sky-blue ranch house.

Three young men, two of them wearing navy slacks and white shirts, get off the bus and walk around to the back of the house, entering the kitchen.

They have ears that stick out and faces that are expressive and filled with energy.

Anthony Melton, 15, is a huge fan of Philadelphia 76ers star Allen Iverson. He drops his book bag and immediately sits down at the table. The youngest brother, 12-year-old Gregory Turner, sits next to him. He is the only brother who has never been in special-education courses and has never had a problem with truancy because he started school while living with Christian.

The third is Dominick Melton, who's 16 years old. Christian describes him as her shadow. When he was much younger, he used to follow her around the house. Though now he's less conspicuous about it, she says, he still wants to make sure he knows where she is. . . .

A "Normal" Family

A calendar hanging on the wall holds myriad coupons and grocery store sales sheets. There are doctor's appointments and notes for the children's DCFS caseworker. Simple requests like: "Mentors," "Tutors," "Swimming Lessons."

Over the years, one of the standing notes has been to ask DCFS to provide tutors, but Christian says that request has gone unanswered.

"I think the state has really failed these kids when it comes to their education," she says. "You can ask and request different things and never see it. I can sit and read to them when

I'm not cooking or doing laundry or stopping a fight. But I don't know how to help them read and comprehend. I feel like this: When the state places them in a halfway decent home, they can't study on them too much." . . .

Gregory, who was just 2 years old at the time of the Keystone incident, says he's embarrassed by it. For him, Keystone is a blur. Much of what he knows is patched together from the memories of his older siblings.

Once, he says he saw a movie about an adopted kid and decided to tell a friend that he was a state ward. But the friend didn't believe him so he decided it was best that nobody knew. "People would start asking questions and I don't want to get into all of that."

"What I want to know is if we can ever go back with our mother?" asks Dominick. He says he doesn't want to leave Christian, but he's tired of having to deal with social workers. "They come here and to the school and everybody knows your business."

"We just want to be normal," says Anthony. He leans forward with clasped hands. . . .

The Birth Mother

Before Keystone, [the brothers' mother, Maxine] Melton's job history consisted of working two days as a secretary, according to state documents. . . . Melton has now worked for nearly four years on an assembly line at a chocolate factory that's walking distance from her home.

Ten years ago, of all the adults in the Keystone apartment, Melton seemed to have the best chance of winning her children back from the system. While incarcerated, she completed parenting and GED classes on her own, and Christian often drove the brothers out to spend time with her. But when she was paroled, several state-mandated evaluations determined that she was unfit to parent. Her parental rights were terminated in 1995.

On the day of Anthony's graduation from elementary school, Melton drives over to Christian's home with balloons and flowers so the family can leave together. During the ceremony in the school's gym, Melton stands in the bleachers waving her balloons. She yells, "That's my baby," when her son's name is called. The entire family applauds as he receives his diploma. Graduations are no small feat in a family where few have high school diplomas. Melton left high school when she was 17 years old and pregnant with Claudell.

Later, when it was time for pictures, Christian and the boys' mother pose at opposite ends of the brothers. In a way the picture represents a metaphor for their relationship. While the women act as counterbalances in the boys' upbringing, they also are at odds at times when it comes to parenting.

Christian says that sometimes Melton gives too much out of guilt. When the brothers spend time with her, they lose ground. They don't have to heed the same rules. They play video games, watch television and don't have to complete chores.

Christian wants her foster sons to know that there are no free rides. They have to work for what they want. "I'm trying to grow them up to be men," Christian says. "They can't afford to be handed everything because somebody's on a guilt trip." . . .

Hopes for the Future

On a recent morning, the Christian home is filled with youngsters. Teenagers sit at the kitchen table playing Monopoly. Younger kids play on the enclosed back porch. . . .

Christian sits in the living room relaxing on a sofa surrounded by the pictures of the boys when they were younger. Hairlines are razor perfect. Smiles are just wide enough to qualify.

For Christian, "What's next?" is not a question she contemplates for too long, she says. She has learned to take life in its smaller increments.

The state is considering asking her to be Claudell's guardian. His difficulties with reading have made it hard for him to get a driver's license and navigate a job application. The caseworker will call soon to make an appointment.

Johnnie Melton is preparing to graduate from high school, and everyone hopes he will be accepted into a small college that offers an equestrian program to nurture his love of horses. Dominick and Anthony will continue on in high school. Next year [2005], Gregory will graduate from elementary school.

She wants her foster sons to move on and create lives for themselves one day. But if they cannot, they will always have a home with her. Though she has given much, she says she has received so much more in return.

Their life is modest but full. She has proven that she will be there for them for as long as she can. Her desires for them are enormous. And, so are their desires for her.

"I want to . . . one day build her a mansion nearby," says Gregory. "That's what I want to do when I grow up."

The Foster Care System Can Contribute to Abuse and Neglect

Leslie Kaufman and Richard Lezin Jones

In the following article, Leslie Kaufman and Richard Lezin Jones report that budget cuts and bureaucratic mismanagement contributed to New Jersey's foster care system being ranked among the worst in the nation by 2003. Over more than a decade, Kaufman and Jones note, the system became increasingly overtaxed when confronted with decreased funding, laid-off caseworkers, and slashed programs for children and parents at risk. With as many as one in five New Jersey foster children being abused, Kaufman and Jones also point to an ineffective and antiquated computer system for tracking children in foster placements and a reliance on voluntary placements with relatives who were not certified or adequately supervised. Leslie Kaufman and Richard Lezin Jones are reporters for the New York Times *who often write about poverty, child abuse, and the child welfare system.*

The admission of government failure could not have been more sweeping. On June 24 [2003], New Jersey, under legal attack and amid a storm of public outcry, agreed to grant broad powers over its child welfare system to outside experts.

By almost every measure, the system was in collapse, often at the brutal cost of children's lives. As many as one in five children in foster care was being abused, and it took years to have imperiled children adopted. New Jersey ranked among the worst in the country, according to child welfare groups, with fully one-quarter of the state's foster children stuck in institutions that national experts have regarded for years as the worst environment.

"We recognized that the system is broken in many places," said Kevin Ryan, an aide to Gov. James E. McGreevey who led the negotiations on turning over control of the system, "and it took a long time to make it as broken as it was."

A System in Collapse

In explaining how New Jersey's care for its most vulnerable children came to be broken so badly and for so long, experts and government officials consistently point to several critical failures: money, staffing and repeated delays in embracing child welfare practices that had succeeded elsewhere in the country.

Across more than a decade—involving both Democratic and Republican administrations—the state engaged in what many claim was a financial retreat involving the kinds of programs deemed by experts to be most essential for protecting children: drug treatment programs for troubled parents, day care for abused children, and a modern computer tracking system that might make it easier for state workers to monitor and manage a growing number of abuse and neglect cases.

At the same time, the state's efforts to keep caseloads down, and to effectively train and support child welfare workers with equipment and expertise, were sporadic and always short-lived.

One administration in Trenton closed the training academy at the Division of Youth and Family Services [DYFS] for six years; another administration cut the number of workers devoted to monitoring the quality of caseworker performance. The State Legislature failed to set limits on the number of cases a worker could be assigned, so that today the average is 41 per worker, as it was a decade ago. Veteran caseworkers say that over the years, the number of staff members assigned to desk jobs has risen, while those assigned to work in the streets and homes where children are at risk are increasingly overwhelmed

Finally, New Jersey took years to adopt and use what for other states had become obvious answers for handling the growing crisis in child welfare. Among them were requiring that foster homes be formally licensed, and placing foster children with relatives rather than strangers—a tactic known as kinship care that many experts believed made for safer and more reliable settings for endangered children.

Indeed, the state's track record of programmatic negligence—in the face of one bad newspaper headline after another and despite multiple expert panel reports—has been so pronounced that the federal judge who approved the takeover by outside experts . . . pledged that he himself would not allow it to happen again.

"What I want to assure the parties on both sides is that for better or for worse, while the political administrations may or may not change, I will be living with this case until it's closed," Judge Stanley R. Chesler said. "I will be going nowhere, and I hope and will do the best I can to make sure that the political will continues to exist to make this settlement become reality, that this is not simply a response to the latest crisis which vanishes when the next crisis appears on the horizon."

Alarming Rises in Caseloads

Looking back on the failure of New Jersey's foster care, one explanation jumps off the pages of the state's budgets. In the last decade, the number of children under the state's care rose alarmingly, to 58,000 from 40,000. Yet for fiscal year 2003, the state's spending on the child welfare agency had barely budged over the 10 years, up only to $312 million from $275 million.

But that modest rise in spending captures only part of the story. The state, in the fiscal years 1995 through 1999, actually cut spending by $67 million despite some of the most robust economic conditions ever.

And to this day, numerous legislators involved in the budget fights cannot explain the repeated collapse of political will

State Senator Diane B. Allen, a Republican who pushed unsuccessfully to spend money to reduce social workers' caseloads, said, "I can't exactly say why we weren't able to do it, except that those constituencies that don't vote have less influence than those that do."

The most marked of the cuts occurred during the administration of Christie Whitman, a Republican who served as governor from 1994 through late January 2001, although Democratic administrations also displayed a disinclination to invest in the child welfare system.

While the agency handles nearly 9,000 more cases annually than it did in 1989, the state has only about 300 more workers to manage them, a result of years of layoffs and what union officials and outside experts say has been inadequate hiring.

Budget Cuts Mean Fewer Social Workers

From 1989 to 1995, the agency lost one out of every six of its caseload-carrying workers, largely because of layoffs initiated by Ms. Whitman and her predecessor, Jim Florio, a Democrat. The move left the agency ill prepared for a four-year period in the mid-1990's when the caseload for most workers rose by more than 13 percent.

The Child Welfare League of America suggests that workers be responsible for no more than 17 cases at one time, a figure that is widely accepted as the national standard. The lower the number of caseloads, experts say, the more time workers can spend with individual children and, in theory, better identify whether they are at risk.

According to state figures, the average caseload for workers in New Jersey is about 41, or more than twice the recommended standard. And, even with Governor McGreevey's promised changes to child welfare under way, officials acknowledge that the number of cases handled by each worker has risen since the beginning of the year.

The cuts, as well, took tools from the hands of the dwindling number of workers, including their cars and cellphones. Even children's car seats were allowed to become scarce

To those who worked both for and with the agency, the late 1990's, with flush general budgets, were particularly demoralizing because, to them, the cuts seemed entirely without

Children that are placed in foster care are supposed to be cared for and protected, but if placed in the wrong home, they frequently end up abused and neglected. © Hannah Gal/ CORBIS.

rationale.

"You would hear someone like the governor saying she wanted to help kids," said Bernice L. Manshel, who was the agency's director until 1982 and then watched as DYFS was dismantled in the subsequent decades.

But, she said, "there was no depth of knowledge or real understanding of the needs."

An Overtaxed, Underfunded System

Perhaps the most searing example of a failure to invest in the system concerned what many current and former government officials regard as the tragedy of the agency's computer system.

In the mid-1990's, the federal government passed a series of sweeping foster care reporting requirements that demanded, among other things, that each state have a centralized database to track foster children or risk losing federal matching funds.

With an ancient computer system, and with many agency offices using half-complete paper files to document cases, New Jersey knew it had to allocate money for the new system as early as 1997, when it actually put up $7 million to buy computers.

In fiscal years 1999, 2000 and 2001, new money to pay for the software and networking for the system was dutifully allocated in the budget. Then, like a slow-motion train wreck, the money was removed at the 11th hour in compromises. The state now says the computers bought in 1997 are out of date anyway.

But for many child welfare workers, and the judges and lawyers who worked with them, almost no budget cut was more counterproductive than the failure to provide the services that might have improved the family conditions for vulnerable children.

The number of residential substance abuse treatment slots specifically for mothers with their children—drug abuse is one of the most frequent factors in child abuse cases—has not increased in the last four years, even as the foster care population took off. Parents struggling with substance abuse often wait months to gain admittance to such treatment programs, advocates for the parents say.

Children, then, were frequently removed and placed in an already overtaxed foster care system.

"The situation is quite desperate," said Nancy Goldhill, vice president and assistant general counsel for Legal Services of New Jersey, which represents parents in cases against the state.

Mismanagement at the Highest Levels

Money alone, of course, does not explain the dizzying decline in the quality of the state's services. Mismanagement and neglect also took their toll.

To run an effective child welfare system, said Ms. Manshel, the former agency director, "it takes sustained interest."

"And at the highest levels of policy making," she said, "there was no real interest."

As a result, experts say, New Jersey was often late—too late—in adopting some of the most basic case practice innovations in child welfare even as they became common in most other states.

It was only in 2001 that New Jersey agreed, for example, to offer foster care stipends to relatives of foster care children who took them in—a step long known to be crucial in poor communities.

"New Jersey was late to recognize kinship care," said Rob Geen, a senior research associate at the Urban Institute, a social policy research group based in Washington. "It really tried to divert kin from any kind of foster care payment, which is discriminatory against relatives. Changes have made for the better, but there are still policies that could be better."

At an even more basic level, officials said, New Jersey went for years without even requiring that foster homes be formally licensed. It was only in 1999, after an astounding amount of abuse was found to be occurring in foster homes, that the state began to do formal certification of homes (it started full licensing in 2002).

To this day, residential facilities are not required to do criminal background checks on their employees. A law mandating such checks is awaiting Governor McGreevey's signature.

Discredited Practices

In a similar sense, New Jersey's failure to abandon some discredited practices, particularly one known as voluntary placement, also set it apart as a distinctly troubled system. Voluntary placement occurs when parents agree to sign their children over to the foster care system—in many cases, parental advocates say, because they believe the child will ultimately be taken away anyway. But those children who are turned over to the state under those circumstances are not afforded the lawyers and other safeguards meant to ensure that the state responsibly handles its case and protects them from harm.

A 1992 report by Legal Services found that 75 percent of children in New Jersey's foster care system were there via voluntary placements, a rate far in excess of any other state.

In the ensuing years, the agency passed regulations limiting the length of time children could remain in such placements without judicial review. Still, the practice continues. As of 2001, the last year for which records were available, there were 2,217 voluntary placements into foster care, or close to half the entire population taken in that year.

Gwendolyn L. Harris, the state's Department of Human Services commissioner, has seen the agency's ills as both a social worker in Newark in the mid-1980's and as the cabinet officer charged by Governor McGreevey with oversight of the agency.

Looking back at what went wrong, she said that the politicians and the public never really understood how dire a situation the agency was in.

"I think there was a lack of political understanding of how severe the problem is," she said. "They'd say, 'We've got to be O.K.' People wanted to believe that we fit somewhere in the middle. That we can't be too bad."

Weighing Children's Safety Against Offenders' Civil Rights

Janet Kornblum

Megan's Law is named for seven-year-old Megan Kanka, a New Jersey girl who was raped and murdered by a convicted sex offender who lived across the street from her home. After her death, her parents founded the Megan Nicole Kanka Foundation and fought for, in the words of the foundation's mission, the right of "every parent . . . to know if a dangerous sexual predator moves into their neighborhood." Megan's Law became a federal law in 1996; it mandates that every state develop a procedure for notifying concerned people when a person convicted of certain crimes—usually sexual assaults and sexual abuse of children—is released back into the community near their homes.

In the following article, Janet Kornblum, a reporter for USA Today, *discusses recent challenges to Megan's Law by civil libertarians and sex offenders, who maintain that the civil rights of the convicted offenders who have served their time, are violated by a public list informing neighbors and potential employers of their criminal history. The article also explores the effectiveness of Megan's law and the difficult issue of balancing offenders' rights with children's safety.*

Sex offenders and civil libertarians have balked at Megan's Law since it was signed in 1996. But it . . . faced its most intense scrutiny in [2003].

In November [2003,] the Supreme Court heard arguments challenging the constitutionality of the law, which requires states to make sex-offender registries available to the public.

The challenge pits the rights of registered sex offenders, who say they have a right to move on with their lives once

Janet Kornblum, "A Tough Balance Between Kids' Safety, Offenders' Rights; Megan's Law Has Critics on Both Sides of Argument," *USA Today,* January 29, 2003, p. D08. Copyright © 2003 by the USA Today Information Network. Reproduced by permission.

they serve their time, against the rights of parents and guardians, who say they need the law to protect their children.

Protecting Civil Rights While Protecting Children

The Supreme Court is considering two separate cases concerning implementation of the law by Alaska and Connecticut. But the ruling also will determine the way other states implement it. A key issue in both cases is whether the law ends up punishing offenders again. [On March 5, 2003, the Supreme Court made it legal for all states to legally place information on registered sex offenders on the Internet.]

The rulings could determine the types of criminals included in the public registries; how the registries are made available to the public (about 31 states put their lists on the Internet); and the process by which a state decides who should be on the list.

The rulings will affect many: As of February 2001, 386,000 convicted sex offenders were on registries throughout the USA, according to the Department of Justice.

The law, named after Megan Kanka, 7, who was raped and murdered in 1994 by a twice-convicted child molester who lived on her block, is also facing the court of public opinion through high-profile news stories.

Two Cases

In Berkeley, Calif., convicted kidnapper and sex offender Kenneth Parnell pleaded not guilty . . . to charges that he tried to buy a child. Neighbors complained that they had no idea of his history; they would have had to go to a local police station and look up records to find out that they were living near an offender.

After this, the Associated Press reported that 44% of California offenders who were supposed to register in the past year failed to do so. "When law enforcement officials search for people who haven't registered in the last year, generally they find half of them where they were last registered," says Mike Van Winkle of the California Department of Justice.

In another recent case, convicted rapist David Siebers, 45, was chased from four states, assaulted and harassed by neighbors after being released from prison.

Critics say the first case demonstrates that Megan's Law isn't always effective and that the Siebers case shows that the list can have direct ramifications.

But the rampant vigilantism that people feared would result from the law has not materialized, says Scott Matson, research associate for the Center for Sex Offender Management, a non-profit project funded by the Department of Justice. He says there are known cases of harassment but few involving violence.

It's Hard to Tell If Megan's Law Works

Critics say that in addition to the civil liberties issues, the law may simply not work. "In some cases it may undermine the ability of some people to reintegrate into the community and make some more at risk rather than less at risk," says Fred Berlin, founder of the Johns Hopkins Sexual Disorders Clinic in Baltimore.

If it were working, "We'd be seeing major drops in sexual offending," says Robert Longo of the New Hope Treatment Center in South Carolina, a private clinic that treats young offenders.

Statistics actually do show that reported incidents of child abuse are dropping, but that drop began before Megan's Law was enacted.

Incidents have been declining 2% to 11% every year from 1992 to 2000, combining for a 40% overall decline, says David Finkelhor, professor of sociology at the University of New Hampshire and director of the Crimes Against Children Research Center.

But it's also impossible to prove the law isn't working.

"How do you measure a negative?" asks Marc Klaas, father of 12-year-old Polly Klaas, who was kidnapped and murdered in 1993.

"Megan's Law is about preventing children from being kidnapped, abused and neglected. So if a child isn't, how do you then make this determination?" he says.

"Megan's Law is all about government having made the decision that the safety of children is of paramount importance—that it is a higher priority than the privacy of the individuals who have committed crimes against children."

Department of Justice Statistics

- About 386,000 convicted sex offenders were registered in 49 states and the District of Columbia as of February 2001, compared with 277,000 in April 1998. (In 2001, Massachusetts was not included; in 1998, Connecticut was not included.)

- California had the largest number of offenders in its registry, with more than 88,000 registrants as of February 2001. (It now has 99,000 offenders, according to the California Department of Justice.) Texas had the second-largest registry in 2001, with almost 30,000 registrants.

- As of February 2001, 29 states and the District of Columbia had searchable Web sites with information on individual sex offenders. Fifteen states had Web sites in 1999, and six states had them in 1998.

The Government Must Invest in Prevention

Thomas L. Birch

In the following selection, which was originally presented in 2004 as testimony before the House Committee on Ways and Means, Thomas L. Birch argues that what the government spends on child abuse prevention and child protection falls far short of what government agencies estimate is needed. He states that treating the problems created by child abuse is not as effective as preventing child abuse in the first place. Rather than spend money addressing the problems of juvenile delinquency, adult criminality, mental illness, substance abuse, and chronic health problems that are the consequences of child abuse, he argues, it would be better to prevent abuse through community-based, in-home services to at-risk families. A range of services, such as voluntary home visits, family support services, parenting education, and respite care, Birch suggests, can work together to create a community plan to prevent child abuse and neglect.

Thomas L. Birch is the legislative counsel for the National Child Abuse Coalition, which consists of twenty-five national organizations working together to focus attention on the protection of children and the prevention of child maltreatment.

When we look at federal, state and local government spending on child welfare services, we see that we are investing in an outcome that no one wants—the placement of children in foster care. We are spending well over $16 billion each year to subsidize the foster care and adoptive placements of children who have been so seriously abused and neglected, so injured and in such danger that they are no longer safe to be left at home with their parents. A fraction of that amount is spent on prevention and intervention services to protect children from such severe harm.

Thomas L. Birch, statement before the U.S. House Subcommittee on Human Resources, Committee on Ways and Means, Washington, DC, January 28, 2004.

No one would argue that we should not be paying to protect the children who have been the most seriously injured. But the fact is that the United States spends billions of dollars on programs that deal with the results of our failure to invest real money to prevent and treat child abuse and neglect.

Because our system is weighted toward protecting the most seriously injured children, we wait until it gets so bad that we have to step in. Far less attention in policy or funding is directed at preventing harm to children from ever happening in the first place or providing the appropriate services and treatment needed by families and children victimized by abuse or neglect.

In 2004, looking at the federal child welfare budget . . . the federal government pays out over $7 billion for out-of-home placements. Contrast that with funds . . . [that] add up to less than $900 million for prevention and intervention services to children and their families. For every federal dollar spent on foster care and adoption subsidies, we spend less than thirteen cents in federal child welfare funding on preventing and treating child abuse and neglect.

It is not enough for the federal government to provide services only for foster care and adoption; we have to put together additional resources to help states and communities build their capacity to support preventive services and treatment services as well. But until we reorder our overall budget priorities and begin allocating significant resources to prevention, we will never stop the flow of children onto our nation's foster care rolls. Putting dollars aside for prevention is sound investing, not luxury spending.

The Spending Gap in Child Welfare Prevention and Protection

When we look at what we should be spending to improve the child protective service system and support community-based programs for preventing child abuse and neglect, we discover an enormous spending gap in prevention and protection.

We have a spending gap in this country of almost $13 billion in services to prevent child abuse and to intervene on behalf of children known to the child protection system. In 2000, spending in federal, state and local dollars for child protective services and preventive services amounts to only about $2.9 billion of the estimated $15.9 billion total cost of what ought to be spent on those services.

According to the Urban Institute, states reported spending $20 billion on child welfare in 2000, and they could categorize how $15.7 billion of the funds were used. Of that amount, $9.1 billion was spent for out-of-home placements, $1.8 billion on administration, $1.9 billion on adoption, and $2.9 billion (about 18 percent) on all other services, including prevention, family preservation and support services, and child protective services. . . .

The Costs of Abuse and Neglect

First, consider the cost to child protective services of 1) investigating the reports of child abuse and neglect that were accepted in 2000 and 2) providing some basic services to the victims of child maltreatment in that year. When we look at the expense of investigating the 1.726 million children who were screened in for further assessment, plus the expense of providing services to the 879,000 substantiated child victims and to the 385,000 children in unsubstantiated reports who also received some services, we come up with a total cost of $5.9 billion.

We should not, here, overlook the unacceptable fact that nearly half the victims of child maltreatment in fact receive no services at all. One of the great tragedies of our system for protecting children is the hundreds of thousands of children—over 392,000 (45%) victims of child abuse in 2000—

who received no services whatsoever: suspected abuse reported, report investigated, report substantiated, case closed. . . .

The CPS [Child Protective Services] spending shortfall amounts to a failure to invest in a system that could successfully protect children from abuse and neglect. When examining the actual dollars spent, the gap in CPS funding—a spending shortfall of nearly $3 billion—must be held accountable for many of the barriers to the adequate protection of children. Failing to invest in a working child protection system results in a national failure to keep children free from harm.

The Failure to Invest in Prevention

Second, consider the cost of preventive services—$10 billion if offered to the three million child maltreatment victims identified in the HHS [Health and Human Services] National Incidence Study III [2002]—and I am not even talking about cost of offering voluntary, universal preventive services to families. That's a total cost of $15.9 billion. Yet, in 2000, states spent only $2.9 billion in federal, state and local funds on protective and preventive services for children. Our national child welfare policy represents a morally unacceptable failure to invest in this system.

These are conservative cost figures. When adjusted to account for inflation, data indicate that investigations by child protective service agencies cost approximately $990 per case. The cost per case to provide basic in-home services such as homemaker assistance or family counseling is $3,295. These costs are low to start with. Pay scales in child welfare are generally low and noncompetitive—significantly lower, for example, than salaries for teachers, school counselors, nurses and public-health social workers—which brings these costs in at an unrealistically low level.

What does the spending gap mean in terms of the child welfare workforce? Ninety percent of states report having difficulty in recruiting and retaining child welfare workers, because of issues like low salaries, high caseloads, insufficient training and limited supervision, and the turnover of child welfare workers—estimated to be between 30 and 40 percent annually nationwide. When we look at caseloads for child welfare workers, the average is double the recommended caseload, and obviously much higher in many jurisdictions.

Prevention Reduces Crime, School Failure

Our present system of treating abused and neglected children and offering some help to troubled families is overworked and inadequate to the task. We need to reorganize the current child protection system to come within the framework of a broader family support system. Hundreds of thousands of children are currently identified as having been abused, but receive no services to prevent further abuse. We must focus attention on children and families known to the system in order to prevent reoccurrence of abuse, as well as provide services to families earlier, before problems become severe.

For more than twenty years, the federal government's attention has concentrated on a restricted approach to child abuse and neglect, in many ways preventing the development of a major federal attack on the problem. As a result, the prevention of child maltreatment of children, which lies at the root of many of this nation's social ills, has been marginalized.

We know that child abuse prevention fights crime, because research has shown us time after time that victims of child abuse are more likely to engage in criminality later in life, that childhood abuse increases the odds of future delinquency and adult criminality overall by 40 percent.

We know that preventing child maltreatment helps to prevent failure in school. Typically abused and neglected children suffer poor prospects for success in school, exhibiting poor initiative, language and other developmental delays, and a disproportionate amount of incompetence and failure. Ensuring that children are ready to learn means ensuring that children are safe at home with the kind of nurturing care that all children deserve.

We know that preventing child abuse can help to prevent disabling conditions in children. Physical abuse of children can result in brain damage, mental retardation, cerebral palsy, and learning disorders.

Prevention Reduces Social Costs of Physical and Mental Illness

Groundbreaking research conducted by the Centers for Disease Control [CDC] in collaboration with [the health group] Kaiser Permanente shows us that childhood abuse is linked with behaviors later in life which result in the development of chronic diseases that cause death and disability, such as heart disease, cancer, chronic lung and liver diseases, and skeletal fracture. Similarly, the CDC research shows that adult victims of child maltreatment are more likely to engage in early first intercourse, have an unintended pregnancy, have high lifetime numbers of sexual partners, and suffer from depression and suicide attempts.

We know that women who suffered serious assaults in childhood experience more episodes of depression, post-traumatic stress, and substance abuse, demonstrating a relationship between childhood trauma and adult psychopathology, as well as links between childhood neglect and later alcohol problems in women.

Finally, looking at the consequences of child maltreatment, we find that among homeless people, many of them, especially homeless women, reported serious family problems or a history of sexual or physical abuse as children that predisposed them to homelessness as adults.

An analysis of the costs of child abuse and neglect in the United States looking at the direct costs of hospitalizations, chronic health problems, mental health care, child welfare services, law enforcement intervention, and the judicial process totals over $24 billion annually. When we add the indirect costs from special education, additional health and mental health care, juvenile delinquency and adult criminality, as well as lost productivity, the total annual cost of child abuse and neglect in the United States amounts to more than $94 billion. We cannot sustain this drain of human and financial capital when we know how to support families and prevent abuse from occurring in the first place.

Investing in Prevention Is Cost Effective

Preventing child abuse is cost effective. Over ten years ago (1992) a report by the General Accounting Office looking at evaluations of child abuse prevention efforts found that "total federal costs of providing prevention programs for low-income populations were nearly offset after four years."

Community-based, in-home services to overburdened families are far less costly than the damage inflicted on children that leads to outlays for child protective services, law enforcement, courts, foster care, health care and the treatment of adults recovering from child abuse. A range of services, such as voluntary home-visiting, family support services, parent mutual support programs, parenting education, and respite care contribute to a community's successful strategy to prevent child abuse and neglect. To be eligible for federal child welfare assistance, states should be required to develop a prevention plan including effective programs identified to carry out the prevention work of community-based programs serving families and children. . . . It is our collective responsibility and our duty to America's children and the nation's future to work toward that goal.

The Child Welfare System Must Be Held Accountable

Carolyn A. Kubitschek

In the following article, Carolyn A. Kubitschek, an attorney with an expertise in foster care and domestic violence, argues that when the state acts in a parental capacity, as it does when a child is placed into foster care, the state is responsible for the child's well-being. She insists that if a child is abused while in foster care, the state must be held accountable. Unfortunately, Kubitschek notes, state agencies are not always being made to account for abused foster children. However, Kubitschek allows that recent court decisions are showing some promise for abused children seeking redress.

Carolyn A. Kubitschek is a partner in the Lansner and Kubitschek law firm in New York City and an adjunct professor at Cardozo School of Law. An expert in family law, she served as the attorney in the case she discusses here, Doe v. New York City Department of Social Services, *which established for the first time that state and foster care agencies are liable for the abuse children suffer while under their care.*

We have all heard some version of the story. [In a February 20, 2001, *New York Daily News* article, Bob Port writes:]

> For half his life, 8-year-old Marcus Smith has had to wear a helmet . . . to protect his brain, which has only the healed skin of his scalp to protect the right side of his head. . . . When he was four, Marcus was beaten unconscious, his skull smashed like an eggshell, leaving his brain bruised and permanently damaged. . . . This would have been more than

enough for city authorities to crash down doors to get the perpetrator, except for one thing: Marcus was a foster child at the time, taken from his mother and entrusted to the care of the city.

The blows that crushed Marcus's skull were allegedly inflicted by a teenage son of Marcus's foster mother. The foster care agency that oversaw Marcus's care had ignored complaints from the boy's mother and grandmother. Indeed, as the newspaper noted, "even as [Marcus] lay in intensive care with a shattered skull, caseworkers submitted an internal report saying he was in good health."

When the government removes children from parents it claims are abusive, neglectful, or unfit, at a minimum the government must place the children in safer environments than those they left. In many cases, this does not happen. Throughout our country, foster children are placed in homes and institutions where they suffer horrendous abuse and neglect, and sometimes even death, at the hands of their purported protectors.

Placing Children in Abusive Foster Homes

"I know that there are good foster families out there, OK?" a former foster child said [in the PBS television documentary, *Frontline: Failure to Protect—A National Dialogue*, first aired on February 6, 2003]. "But I also know that every foster kid that I have ever talked to, including myself, has been abused in foster homes." In New Jersey, the system has deteriorated to the point that Marsha Robinson Lowry, executive director of Children's Rights, Inc., concluded that "it is now a documented fact that no child is safe today in [the state's] foster care."

Our nation's most vulnerable children deserve better. Having been removed from their homes and families—and often from their neighborhoods, friends, schools, and religious institutions—they are helpless and at the mercy of the agencies that are charged with providing substitute care. All too often, foster care agencies fail at their job. Government social workers also habitually fall short. Some children languish for years in abusive situations while the officials charged with protecting them either do not know what is going on or choose to see no evil, hear no evil, speak no evil, and write no evil in the case file.

Placing foster children in abusive homes is appalling. Failing to protect them, so that the abuse continues, is inexcusable. It is also unconstitutional. The U.S. Supreme Court has repeatedly ruled that people who are in government custody have a constitutional right to safe conditions during confinement and protection from injuries inflicted by others. The Court has extended its ruling to prisoners, suspects in jail awaiting trial, and involuntarily hospitalized mental patients. The Court has not yet decided whether foster children have the same right to protection as prisoners, criminal suspects, and mental patients. However, nine federal judicial circuits have ruled that foster children, who are innocent of any wrongdoing, are at least entitled to the same constitutional protections, in terms of safe conditions of confinement, as convicted felons. When foster care agencies fail to provide those protections, they may be held liable.

Court Rulings Can Help Abused Foster Children

The constitutional rulings have provided some redress for abused foster children. They may sue under 42 U.S.C. section 1983 to obtain compensation from the agencies that have wronged them. Importantly, the Constitution, as the supreme law of the land, trumps all state statutes and case law that might give full or partial sovereign immunity to government agencies or employees, or that might impose procedural prerequisites on children asserting claims against state or local governments. However, the law falls far short of providing a remedy for comprehensive damages for all abused foster children. Numerous hurdles remain for an abused foster child.

First, in states that provide foster care directly through a statewide program, the government agencies themselves are immune from suit in federal court under the Eleventh Amendment. (Where foster care is provided by counties or other local governments—as in New York, California, and some other states—the Eleventh Amendment does not prohibit lawsuits.) In all states, agency employees and officials may still be sued, however.

Second, in all lawsuits under 42 U.S.C. section 1983, the standard of liability is much higher than the negligence standard of tort law. Foster care agencies, officials, and employees will not be held to account unless their behavior exhibits "deliberate indifference" to a risk of harm to the foster children[, as demonstrated in *Doe v. New York City Department of Social Services*]. This heightened standard of liability has been exploited by careless foster care agencies to avoid legal consequences of their careless mistakes.

Legally Holding Agencies Accountable for Abuse

A third problem for abused foster children seeking legal recourse is the issue of proximate cause. As in tort law, defendants are responsible for the consequences of only those injuries that they cause. Foster care agencies and staff do not normally abuse foster children directly. The abuse is usually inflicted by foster parents and family members, or other foster children in the household. The courts have held that foster care agencies will be liable for abuse inflicted by foster parents when the agencies' behavior was a "substantial factor" leading to the abuse. If the chain of causation is found to be too attenuated, however, the agency will escape liability.

Finally, 42 U.S.C. section 1983 contains its own defense. All defendants can potentially claim the defense of qualified immunity and avoid paying damages if their actions or omissions violated a law that was not clearly established at the time, or if their actions or omissions were objectively reasonable, as determined by the judge (not the jury). While agencies themselves cannot claim qualified immunity, their employees can, and the employees have avoided compensating abused foster children by using that defense.

Despite all the hurdles, many abused foster children can and do obtain compensation. Three years after his injury, Marcus has twice undergone surgery on his skull. A permanent plate has replaced his helmet and, except for the large scars on his head, Marcus looks like any other child. He is doing well in his special education class at school. When he turns eighteen, he will begin to receive a monthly annuity out of the $1.25 million settlement of his lawsuit for the abuse he suffered in foster care. That sum in theory replaces the salary that Marcus will unfortunately never be able to earn.

Organizations to Contact

ACT for Kids
210 W. Sprague Ave., Spokane, WA 99201
(866) 348-KIDS (5437) • fax: (509) 747-0609
e-mail: resources@actforkids.org
Web site: www.actforkids.org

ACT for Kids is a nonprofit organization that provides resources, consultation, research, and training for the prevention and treatment of child abuse and sexual violence. In addition to videotapes and therapeutic games, the organization markets workbooks; manuals; books for abused children, including *My Very Own Book About Me*, *Telling Isn't Tattling*, and *It Happens to Boys, Too*; and books for parents such as *How to Survive the Sexual Abuse of Your Child* and *Understanding Children's Sexual Behaviors: What's Natural and Healthy*.

American Academy of Child and Adolescent Psychiatry (AACAP)
3615 Wisconsin Ave. NW, Washington, DC 20016-3007
(202) 966-7300 • fax: (202) 966-2891
Web site: www.aacap.org

AACAP supports and advances child and adolescent psychiatry through research and the distribution of information. The academy's goal is to provide information that will ensure proper treatment for children who suffer from mental or behavioral disorders due to child abuse, molestation, or other factors. AACAP publishes fact sheets on a variety of issues concerning disorders that may affect children and adolescents.

American Professional Society on the Abuse of Children (APSAC)
PO Box 30669, Charleston, SC 29417
(877) 40A-PSAC (2-7722) • fax: (803) 753-9823

e-mail: apsac@comcast.net
Web site: www.apsac.org

APSAC is a nonprofit organization dedicated to improving the coordination of services for professionals in the fields of child abuse prevention, treatment, and research. It publishes the quarterly newsletter *APSAC Advisor* and produces manuals such as *Psychosocial Evaluation of Suspected Sexual Abuse in Children*.

False Memory Syndrome Foundation
1955 Locust St., Philadelphia, PA 19103
(215) 940-1040 • fax: (215) 940-1042
Web site: www.fmsfonline.org

The foundation believes that many "delayed memories" of sexual abuse are the result of false memory syndrome (FMS), which is exhibited when patients in therapy "recall" childhood abuse that never occurred. The foundation seeks to discover the real reasons for the spread of FMS, works for the prevention of new cases, and aids FMS victims, including those falsely accused of abuse. The foundation publishes a newsletter and various papers and distributes articles and information on FMS.

**The Leadership Council on Child Abuse &
Interpersonal Violence**
191 Presidential Blvd., Suite C-132,
 Bala Cynwyd, PA 19004
(610) 664-5007 • fax: (610) 664-5279
e-mail: desk@leadershipcouncil.org
Web site: www.leadershipcouncil.org

The Leadership Council on Child Abuse & Interpersonal Violence is a nonprofit, independent scientific organization composed of scientists, clinicians, educators, legal scholars, and public policy analysts. The Leadership Council seeks to correct the misuse of psychological science to serve vested interests or justify victimizing vulnerable populations—especially abused and neglected children.

National Center for Missing & Exploited Children (NCMEC)

Charles B. Wang International Children's
 Center, Alexandria, VA 22314–3175
(703) 274-3900 • fax: (703) 274-2200
Web site: www.missingkids.com

NCMEC serves as a clearinghouse of information on missing and exploited children and coordinates child protection efforts with the private sector. A number of publications on these issues are available, including guidelines for parents whose children are testifying in court and help for abused children. In 2001, NCMEC launched the NetSmartz program to teach children about Internet safety.

National Clearinghouse on Child Abuse and Neglect Information

1250 Maryland Ave. SW, 8th Fl.
 Washington, DC 20024
(703) 385-7565 • fax: (703) 385-3206
e-mail: nccanch@caliber.com
Web site: http://nccanch.acf.hhs.gov

This national clearinghouse collects, catalogs, and disseminates information on all aspects of child maltreatment, including identification, prevention, treatment, public awareness, training, and education. The clearinghouse offers various reports, fact sheets, and bulletins concerning child abuse and neglect. *The Children's Bureau Express* is an online publication for professionals involved in child abuse and neglect, child welfare, and adoption.

National Coalition Against Domestic Violence (NCADV)

PO Box 18749, Denver, CO 80918
(303) 389-1852 • fax: (303) 831-9251
e-mail: mainoffice@ncadv.org
Web site: www.ncadv.org

It is the mission of NCADV to work for major societal changes necessary to eliminate both personal and societal violence against all women and children. NCADV addresses issues affecting children who witness violence at home or are themselves abused. It publishes the *Bulletin*, a quarterly newsletter.

National Criminal Justice Reference Service (NCJRS)
U.S. Department of Justice, Rockville, MD 20849
(301) 519-5500 • fax: (301) 519-5212
Web site: www.ncjrs.gov

A research and development agency of the U.S. Department of Justice, NCJRS was established to prevent and reduce crime and to improve the criminal justice system. Among its many publications are *Resource Guidelines: Improving Court Practice in Child Abuse and Neglect Cases* and *Recognizing When a Child's Injury or Illness Is Caused by Abuse* .

National Data Archive on Child Abuse and Neglect (NDACAN)
Beebe Hall—FLDC, Cornell University
   Ithaca, NY 14853
(607) 255-7799 • fax: (607) 255-8562
e-mail: NDACAN@cornell.edu
Web site: www.ndacan.cornell.edu

The mission of the National Data Archive on Child Abuse and Neglect is to facilitate the secondary analysis of research data relevant to the study of child abuse and neglect. By making data available to a larger number of researchers, NDACAN seeks to provide a relatively inexpensive and scientifically productive means for researchers to explore important issues in the child maltreatment field. Recent NDACAN data sets include *Longitudinal Pathways to Resilience in Maltreated Children, Adoption and Foster Care Analysis and Reporting System (AFCARS), National Child Abuse and Neglect Data System (NCANDS), Longitudinal Studies of Child Abuse and Neglect (LONGSCAN)*, and *The National Survey of Child and Adolescent Well-Being (NSCAW)*.

Prevent Child Abuse America (PCAA)
200 S. Michigan Ave., 17th Fl.
  Chicago, IL 60604-2404
(312) 663-3520 • fax: (312) 939-8962
e-mail: mailbox@preventchildabuse.org
Web site: www.preventchildabuse.org

PCAA's mission is to prevent all forms of child abuse. It distributes and publishes materials on a variety of topics, including child abuse and child abuse prevention. *Talking About Child Sexual Abuse* and *Basic Facts About Child Sexual Abuse* are among the various pamphlets PCAA offers.

The Rape, Abuse & Incest National Network (RAINN)
635-B Pennsylvania Ave. SE
  Washington, DC 20003
(202) 544-1034 • fax: (202) 544-1401
e-mail: info@rainn.org
Web site: www.rainn.org

The Rape, Abuse & Incest National Network is the nation's largest antisexual assault organization. RAINN operates the National Sexual Assault Hotline and carries out programs to prevent sexual assault, help victims, and ensure that rapists are brought to justice. Their Web site contains statistics, counseling resources, prevention tips, news, and more.

The Recovered Memory Project
Taubman Center for Public Policy and
  American Institutions at Brown University
  Providence, RI 02912
(401) 863-2201
e-mail: ross_cheit@brown.edu
Web site: www.brown.edu/Departments/
Taubman_Center/Recovmem

The purpose of the Recovered Memory Project is to collect and disseminate information relevant to the debate over whether traumatic events can be forgotten and then remembered later in life. That debate has focused on recovered memories of childhood sexual abuse. But the phenomenon extends to other traumas, including physical abuse or witnessing a murder. The Web site collects cases that support the project's viewpoint, including clinical studies and work by cognitive psychologists. It also offers resources for survivors of trauma.

The Safer Society Foundation
PO Box 340, Brandon, VT 05733-0340
(802) 247-3132 • fax: (802) 247-4233
Web site: www.safersociety.org

The Safer Society Foundation is a national research, advocacy, and referral center for the prevention of sexual abuse of children and adults. The Safer Society Press publishes research, studies, and books on treatment for sexual abuse victims and offenders and on the prevention of sexual abuse.

Survivor Connections
52 Lyndon Rd., Cranston, RI 02905-1121
e-mail: survivorconnections@cox.net
Web site: http://members.cox.net/survivorconnections

Survivor Connections is an activist center for survivors of incest, rape, sexual assault, and child molestation. Survivor Connections publishes the online newsletter *Survivor Activist*.

Bibliography

Books

Michael Bannon and Yvonne Carter
Protecting Children from Abuse and Neglect in Primary Care. New York: Oxford University Press, 2003.

Kevin Browne et al., eds.
Early Prediction and Prevention of Child Abuse: A Handbook. New York: John Wiley & Sons, 2002.

Cynthia Crosston-Tower
Understanding Child Abuse and Neglect. Boston: Pearson/A&B, 2005.

Karen A. Duncan
Healing from the Trauma of Childhood Sexual Abuse: The Journey for Women. Westport, CT: Praeger, 2004.

Andrew Durham
Young Men Surviving Child Sexual Abuse: Research Stories and Lessons for Therapeutic Practice. New York: John Wiley & Sons, 2003.

David France
Our Fathers: The Secret Life of the Catholic Church in an Age of Scandal. New York: Broadway, 2005.

Julie Gregory
Sickened: The Memoir of a Munchausen by Proxy Childhood. New York: Bantam, 2003.

Denise A. Hines and Kathleen Malley-Morrison
Family Violence in the United States: Defining, Understanding, and Combating Abuse. Thousand Oaks, CA: Sage, 2005.

Roger J.R.
Levesque

Child Maltreatment Law: Foundations in Science, Practice, and Policy. Durham, NC: Carolina Academic Press, 2002.

NCH Children
and Families
Project

Creating a Safe Place: Helping Children and Families Recover from Child Sexual Abuse. Philadelphia: Jessica Kingsley, 2001.

James R.
Peinkofer

Silenced Angels: The Medical, Legal, and Social Aspects of Shaken Baby Syndrome. Westport, CT: Auburn House, 2002.

Richard B. Pelzer

A Brother's Journey: Surviving a Childhood of Abuse. New York: Warner, 2005.

Dorothy
Rabinowitz

No Crueler Tyrannies: Accusation, False Witness, and Other Terrors of Our Times. New York: Wall Street Journal Books, 2003.

Maria
Scannapieco

Understanding Child Maltreatment: An Ecological and Developmental Perspective. New York: Oxford University Press, 2005.

Murray A. Straus
with Denise A.
Donnelly

Beating the Devil Out of Them: Corporal Punishment in American Families and Its Effects on Children. New Brunswick, NJ: Transaction, 2001.

Julie Taylor and
Brigid Daniel,
eds.

Child Neglect: Practice Issues for Health and Social Care. London: Jessica Kingsley, 2004.

Periodicals

Michael J. Bader	"Who Is Hurting the Children? The Political Psychology of Pedophilia in American Society," *Tikkun*, May/June 2003.
Daniel Bergner	"The Making of a Molester," *New York Times Magazine*, January 23, 2005.
Agostino Bono	"Dealing with the Pain: Bishops and Abuse Victims Meet," *America*, November 17, 2003.
Stephanie Booth	"She Threw Her Baby Away," *Teen People*, May 2002.
Patricia Chisholm	"Who Decides What's Right?" *Maclean's*, September 10, 2001.
Cornelia Cornell	"Don't Touch: Have We Gone Too Far to Protect Our Kids from Inappropriate Contact?" *Today's Parent*, July 2001.
Christopher Earls	"Understanding Child Molesters," *Archives of Sexual Behavior*, December 2002.
Nikitta A. Foston	"The Shocking Story Behind the Pain Nobody Talks About: Sexual Abuse of Black Boys," *Ebony*, June 2005.
Brenda Goodman	"Forgiveness Is Good, Up to a Point: Some Abuse Victims Should Not Reconcile with Abusers," *Psychology Today*, January/February 2004.

Jan Goodwin	"Why Can't We Protect Our Children?" *Family Circle*, April 3, 2001.
Kathryn Harley	"Baby John's Mysterious Malady," *Reader's Digest*, January 2001.
Jerry Harris	"Drug-Endangered Children," *FBI Law Enforcement Bulletin*, February 2004.
J.D. Heyman et al.	"Did Bullying—or a Mother's Neglect—Drive a 12-Year-Old Boy to Suicide?" *People*, October 20, 2003.
Mary C. Hickey	"The Tragedy of Shaken Baby Syndrome," *Parents*, November 2001.
Gay Jervey	"The Bad Mother," *Good Housekeeping*, August 2004.
Maggie Jones	"Who Was Abused?" *New York Times Magazine*, September 19, 2004.
Rivka Gerwitz Little	"Who's Minding the Kids?" *Village Voice*, March 25, 2003.
Bob Meadows et al.	"Two Little Girls Lost, Two Tragic Endings," *People*, April 4, 2005.
Marguerite Michaels	"A Church Plan on Sex Abuse," *Time*, November 25, 2002.
Ami Neiberger-Miller	"Exposing a Dark Secret," *Children's Voice*, March/April 2004.
Thomas P. Rausch	"Where Do We Go from Here?" *America*, October 18, 2004.

Sharon Secor   "Foster Care Crisis: Let the Numbers
                        Speak," *Everybody's*, July/August 2004.

Clare Sheridan   "If Only You Hadn't, I Would Not
and Nancy Wolfe   Have Hit You: Infant Crying and
                        Abuse," *Lancet*, October 9–15, 2004.

Suzanne Smalley   "Suffer the Children," *Newsweek*,
and Brian Braiker   January 20, 2003.

Margaret Talbot   "The Bad Mother: A Reporter at
                        Large," *New Yorker*, August 9, 2004.

Martin H.   "Scars That Won't Heal: The Neuro-
Teichner   biology of Child Abuse," *Scientific
                        American*, March 2002.

Alex Tresniowski   "Monsters or Misjudged?" *People*,
                        November 24, 2003.

Steve Twedt   "The Fearful Flip Side of Child Pro-
                        tection," *Youth Today*, December
                        2004/January 2005.

Terry Donovan   "A Victim's Defense of Priests," *Com-
Urekew   monweal*, October 11, 2002.

Tina Wright   "Stopping the Cycle of Abuse," *Black
                        Parenting*, June 30, 2001.

Index